CURIOUS ABOUT CULTURE

CURIOUS
about
CULTURE

**Refocus your lens on culture to
cultivate cross-cultural understanding**

Gaiti Rabbani

First published in 2021 by Major Street Publishing Pty Ltd
E: info@majorstreet.com.au W: majorstreet.com.au M: +61 421 707 983

The moral rights of the author have been asserted.

 A catalogue record for this book
is available from the National Library
of Australia

NATIONAL
LIBRARY
OF AUSTRALIA

Printed book ISBN: 978-0-6489803-0-8
Ebook ISBN: 978-0-6489803-1-5

CQ is a registered trademark of the Cultural Intelligence Center.

Cover design by Simone Geary
Internal design by Production Works
Printed in Australia by Ovato, an Accredited ISO AS/NZS 14001:2004
Environmental Management System Printer.

10 9 8 7 6 5 4 3 2 1

CONTENTS

Curiosity

To be curious is to seek knowledge. Curiosity is a quality related to inquisitive thinking, exploration and learning. It arises when we notice a gap in our knowledge and understanding. I sincerely hope that the insights in *Curious about Culture* will go some way in quenching your thirst for that knowledge.

PREFACE

If you have picked up this book, chances are that you are curious about culture. Whether you travel abroad or stay at home, whether you work and live in the northern hemisphere or in the south, the likelihood of interacting with someone of a different cultural background is very high. Those probabilities are multiplied a few fold here in the richly diverse peoplescape of Australia.

What does culture mean to you? How would you describe the characteristics of your culture? When we speak of culture most people think of ethnicity and nationality. In reality, however, culture transcends racial and geographical boundaries. It is not only about where we were born, who we were born to and where we live. Gender, generation and language among other factors also contribute to how we interact with the social landscape around us.

We are all members of more than one culture. We identify with several cultures through our personal and professional selves – family, community, national and organisational just to name a few. We may act differently depending on which cultural dimension we wish to express or which cultural group we are interacting with at any given time. I may think of myself as a woman, a business entrepreneur, a teacher, an English speaker or a global citizen.

Our expression in life, at work and at play, is honed through our uniquely personal culture. Each one of us is shaped by multiple and complex layers of culture to form our cultural identities. There are many dimensions that construct our individual identities and define what is intrinsically important to us, shaping our perception of the world around us.

With the acknowledgement that culture is stratified, the purpose of this book is to help you peel back the multi-faceted layers of culture. Through the chapters of this book, we will deconstruct the broad-brush approach that has become synonymous with the word 'culture'. I will encourage you to be curious, to expand your cultural awareness and to develop cultural sensitivity. Often the fear of saying the 'wrong' thing or offending someone can be stifling. I will offer suggestions on how to frame your curiosity and initiate cross-cultural dialogue with confidence.

Are you looking to uncover your own cultural drivers? Are you seeking to connect with cultural strangers? Are you looking for tools to navigate a multicultural landscape? Whatever your motivation for reading this book, it will lead you to some deep and valuable insights.

Cross-cultural encounters

On any given day we interact with people across a spectrum of cultures. Allow me to share a slice of my everyday life as a frame of reference.

On a typical morning I wake to a host of messages from family, friends and clients across the time zones: a rushed WhatsApp note from a client in Dubai whose inflated sense of urgency makes everything appear a matter of life or death; a cheery email from a client across the harbour in Sydney (I'm convinced I'm the first person she talks to every morning and the last person she messages at night!); hurried messages from my sister in the north of England, carrying updates of my mum who is struggling to adapt to her new care home; a series of endearing emoticons as substitute hugs from friends in Istanbul; and a spirited Facebook message from my early bird daughter in Queensland boasting about a new beachside café she has discovered on her sunrise walk, and reminding me to check my Insta account.

Invigorated by my L'Occitane verbena-infused shower I attempt to respond to all incoming communications, urgent or not, whether the recipients are awake or not. In the background, I hear my Sri Lankan partner asking if I've seen his spectacles. I can't help but giggle. 'Spectacles' – really?

My morning continues with a ritual-esque stroll to my local café, Garcon. Sam the manager greets me with a welcoming smile and a nod of the head that says, 'I know what you want…' A couple of taps on his iPad and my order is magically transmitted to the trusted hands of my barista, Kelvin, who hails from Indonesia.

How many cultures have I encountered, all before the first sip of my Colombian deep-roasted blend?

I am straddling the obvious diversity that resides across national borders – England, the United Arab Emirates (UAE), Turkey, Sri Lanka and Indonesia. My story alludes to a European influence with my penchant for French brands. I find myself navigating the digital divide across all possible messaging media that I can keep up with, appeasing my daughter via Facebook (after checking Insta!) and my clients via email and WhatsApp. My style changes from the professional 'down-to-business' to the friendly and relaxed, in response to the tone of my clients. I find my partner's spectacles and I hand them back with a reminder that no-one uses that colonial term anymore!

From generation to gender to language, I have effectively circumvented any potential cultural collisions and I am ready to savour my morning coffee.

I can't pretend that I fully understand the beliefs, the attitudes, the values or the norms that each of these cultural groups holds dear. What I have come to learn is that sensitivity to the cultural orientations of others plays a big part in my own success at fostering meaningful relationships.

How many cross-cultural interactions feature in your daily encounters – at home, at work and in your day to day life? Your daily interactions may not traverse national boundaries or international time zones; however, you don't have to cross geographical borders to face a culturally nuanced situation: Australia's domestic population is one of the most culturally and linguistically diverse in the world. A country of immigrants, Australia's people come from over 190 nations, and more than 75 per cent of the nation identifies with an ancestry other than Australian. A third of Australia's population was born overseas. Through the 7.5 million migrants living in Australia, every single country from around the world was represented in Australia's population in 2019. Over 300 separately identified languages are spoken in Australian homes while more than one-fifth of Australians speak a language other than English at home. We also have four to five generations in the workplace.

How's that for cultural diversity?

About this book

The ease with which we connect and maintain personal and professional relationships is influenced by the lens through which we view others. To connect across cultures with people of diverse backgrounds, we first need to understand the values that mould our own lens of the world. To improve interpersonal effectiveness in any sphere of our lives we need to look within, understand ourselves and venture into the deeper subconscious patterns of our minds.

In an era of instant gratification our minds seek quick fixes and ready-made solutions – 'just tell me how to do it'. In reality, each situation is unique; every one of us is different; every cross-cultural encounter is underpinned by different dynamics. To be prescriptive would not do justice to the cultural nuances that sway our thinking and behaviour.

The cover of this book features kaleidoscopic glasses – for good reason. You might recall being mesmerised with the colourful images returned through the lens of a kaleidoscope in your childhood days. Much time can be spent entertained by the continuously changing patterns reflected through this simple device. The designs seen through the lens are unique to the viewer. The phenomenon is merely a play of light through angled mirrors reflecting, typically, on a collection of ordinary beads or glass pieces. By rotating the lens, the images seamlessly merge and transform into new and intriguing shapes.

You may be wondering what this has to do with culture. The way we view culture is unique to each of us. The filters that we are about to discover in *Curious about Culture* act as the mirrors. For the viewer who peers through the kaleidoscope, there are several ways to interpret what is seen. Often our vision is blurred through preconceptions informed by our own experience of culture. Culture is not static; like the ever-changing images seen through a kaleidoscope, it is dynamic.

Ultimately, we all view the world differently. We view people differently. We perceive cultural identities differently. We can learn to appreciate this uniqueness. It is fitting that the word 'kaleidoscope' comes from the Greek language and literally means 'observer of beautiful things'.

To sum it up, I use the words of Henry David Thoreau:

> *The question is not what you look at, but what you see.*

Based on my experience as a cultural specialist, a teacher and a coach, this book brings together many parts of my own professional life. I am passionate about facilitating self-awareness among the people I work with, helping them be the best versions of themselves. Consequently, the tone of this book assumes a coaching mindset – one that continuously inspires introspection. I encourage you to reflect on the perspectives offered and consider how they may apply to you. I believe that delivering insights that have personal relevance will be more powerful than 'telling' you what to do.

Curious about Culture offers opportunities to reflect through introspective questions and, where appropriate, provides you with some suggestions to facilitate cross-cultural connection. *Curious about Culture* is designed to be digestible yet impactful. Each main chapter concludes with a 'Be curious' section, offering questions for self-reflection or suggestions to frame your curiosity. Through a series of intentional questions, you can boost your awareness, enhance your personal effectiveness and cultivate your confidence to start meaningful cross-cultural conversations. To access all the 'Be curious' sections in a single worksheet, refer to the exclusive online toolkit at: **rabbanicollective.com/curiousaboutculture**. Please use the password 'I am curious' when prompted.

Part I of this book will help you to build awareness of your own cultural outlook. By uncovering the beliefs and assumptions that are held in your subconscious mind you can deepen your understanding of yourself and how you express yourself in the world. You will start to recognise the invisible lines that have potential to create rifts in multicultural interactions.

In **part II** we examine six themes of culture: gender, generation, faith, education, language and nationality. Each of these cultural filters shapes cultural identities and influences our behaviour. Once you start to understand the principles that distinguish you and those around you, you can begin to shine a light on your blind spots and recognise the impact of bias on judgements when engaging across cultures. You can choose to dive beyond the apparent cues and clues when interacting with diverse people. You can become clearer about where you are projecting your own values and recognise where you could be more understanding of those who seem to differ.

It would be unreasonable to expect you to master all possible cultural nuances that influence your own outlook and that of others. In truth, you don't need to. In **part III** of *Curious about Culture*, I will provide you with a values framework that will help you determine your personal culture orientations against six key dimensions: identity, authority, expression, communication, rules and achievement. As a certified professional with the Cultural Intelligence Center, I draw upon their model to help you decipher the cultural conditioning that may be influencing your perspectives and interactions with others. Learning to navigate these six cultural dimensions will empower you to build stronger connections and bridge previously obscure differences with those of different cultural backgrounds.

Part IV of *Curious about Culture* wraps up with some actionable suggestions on how you might apply this refined lens on cultural understanding. With the intention of boosting your cross-cultural effectiveness, you can learn how to identify and address cultural themes in your workplace.

***

Now that you have reached the end of this preface, you have already started your journey of cross-cultural reflection. If you wish to expand your knowledge further you can do so by downloading an exclusive resource of templates available only to readers of this book from the online toolkit (please see details on page 141).

PART I
CULTURE

I n part I of *Curious about Culture*, I will define the meaning of culture to arrive at a common understanding for the context of this book. I will go on to share some perspectives drawn from some deep and personal experiences. It is my hope that my examples prompt you to recognise your own preconceptions about cultural identities that are different to your own. This is where the journey of developing cultural intelligence begins.

THE CULTURAL QUOTIENT

In this book, I use the phrase 'cultural quotient' to describe our cultural perceptiveness. In academic circles, and now increasingly so in the business world, CQ[1] is the term used to describe cultural intelligence. As with other forms of intelligence, namely IQ and EQ (emotional intelligence), CQ is measurable and can be developed over time.

What is culture?

Culture can be ubiquitous yet simultaneously abstract. We come across the word 'culture' several times a day in different contexts. Let's start by defining it for the setting of this book.

Earlier I walked you through the start of my day, embracing the urban coffee culture as well as the diversity of cultures I frequently navigate. Culture is a multifaceted concept that essentially influences every aspect of our lives – both consciously

---

1   The abbreviation CQ™ is a registered trademark of the Cultural Intelligence Center.

and subconsciously. In its broadest sense culture is a cultivated behaviour.

Social psychologist Geert Hofstede defined culture as 'the collective programming of the mind that distinguishes the members of one category of people from another'. In a nutshell, then, culture is the shared beliefs, traditions, values and identities of a group. Culture is a group phenomenon – one that is learned and experienced through the norms and expectations of a group.

Think about the last time you joined a new organisation or partnered with a company that was proud to take you on an orientation of the business. As you familiarised yourself with the organisational culture you would have gained an understanding of the underlying principles that guide the behaviours of team members with one another, and with the outside world. Essentially, they were communicating their terms of engagement: 'this is the way we do things around here'.

When you pick up a guidebook to plan a holiday, it outlines social norms and customary practices in your destination of choice – religion, dress, language, law, music, arts, holidays and so on. That's simply the way they do things there, as defined by their local culture.

In retail training programs, I occasionally introduce an exercise called 'welcoming someone into your home'. This sets up a conversation about how we greet customers as they enter a boutique environment, compared to how we receive guests at home. The comparison usually opens up an unintended but interesting cross-cultural dialogue. Some participants believe that it is customary to show guests around their house. Some feel that it is an invasion of privacy, and would neither show nor expect to be shown around. Others would do so only if their guest is staying overnight.

What is socially acceptable in one cultural group may not be in another. When someone does something differently to what we may be used to, it appears strange to us – but it is perfectly normal to them. These social norms become cultural quirks that often distinguish one group from another.

A cultural group traverses national borderlines. Christians and Buddhists are cultural groups. Corporations and academia have separate cultural identities. Roles within these organisations such as teachers and leaders have distinctive cultural traits. Sliced differently, gender defines cultural groupings. In collectivist cultures, family is the strongest unit; in individualist cultures, the personal culture prevails.

Personal culture is shaped by factors beyond nationality and the environment in which we live, but also by family and communities. Our cultural narratives start taking form during childhood, from the multiple layers of culture we experience in society. We learn the norms of the cultures we are exposed to, and these learned ideas become integral to our personal value system.

The culture iceberg

We often refer to the iceberg analogy to illustrate the concept of culture. Developed by anthropologist Edward T Hall in the 1970s, the model showcases the depth and breadth of culture – likening the complexity of culture to an iceberg. You can see the top 10 per cent of an iceberg while 90 per cent of its mass sits below the waterline, out of sight. Culture is much the same; the visible layer is a very thin slice.

The proverbial tip of the iceberg accounts for a small part of the cultural mass and represents features that can be expressed and observed easily when we first interact with a new culture – food, dress, social etiquette, traditions, celebrations and behaviour.

If you have ever lived or worked in a different culture, you will know that adapting to local customs, embracing local tastes and observing social etiquette is enriching. These characteristics are an important expression of culture, but can also be adopted without fundamentally compromising people's intrinsic cultural identity.

The remaining 90 per cent of the culture iceberg is submerged below the surface and comprises deep-rooted ideas such as values, beliefs and assumptions. It's like a subliminal framework of rules. Sitting in the subconscious mind, these learned ideas become our cultural conditioning – what is right or wrong, acceptable or not – and dictate the way we behave and communicate, and the choices we make. These core values are difficult to change. They are a fundamental element of our cultural DNA – the multiple dimensions of our unique cultural identities – and asking someone to act outside of their belief system will create a great deal of conflict.

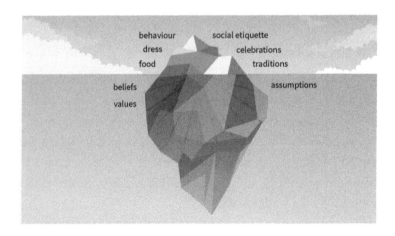

Initially, when two people from different cultures come together, they observe the visible features of culture. In some cultures, including Australia, it is a sign of respect to look someone in the eye when they speak to you. It demonstrates active listening and assures the speaker that you are engaged and interested. In return, if the other person holds eye contact it signals confidence in what is being said. In many Asian cultures, however, it is polite to hold eye contact only briefly – especially in situations where the listener may be of a higher social status. Sporadic meeting of the eyes indicates respect rather than a lack of interest.

Consider a cross-cultural business negotiation. If each person relies only on the observable behaviour – in this case, eye contact – it will most likely trigger mutual feelings of mistrust or a question of respect. While different cultural groups may share the same underlying values such as respect and trust, with this example we can see that the expression of these values can differ.

The iceberg model highlights why we cannot judge a new culture purely on what we see. Instinctively we know there's more to a situation than we initially perceive. Take a moment to consider what happens when someone's behaviour goes against your cultural norms. Did you perceive the other person's behaviour as unacceptable? Disrespectful? Was your perception true? It is essential to take time to uncover the beliefs that underlie the behaviour.

The word 'culture' derives from a French term, which in turn derives from the Latin *colere*, which means to tend to the earth and grow, or cultivate and nurture. I encourage you to cultivate your curiosity and discover how your cultural lens on the world can influence your interactions with people of diverse cultural backgrounds.

Why does it matter?

We are living in an increasingly diverse global community. More often, we are being called on to work, learn and teach in situations where there is more than one culture at play. Research demonstrates that cultural intelligence may easily be the single greatest difference between thriving in the 21st-century world and becoming obsolete.

Acquiring the knowledge, skills and experience necessary to manoeuvre effectively in multicultural environments is increasingly important. Our social landscape comprises diverse societies. Riddled with religious, ethical and language complexities, our complex ecosystem calls for cultural sensitivity. Navigating our interconnected world without collision is key.

People with strong cultural awareness can adapt to others who might perceive the world differently. Developing your cultural sensitivity offers the pathway to navigating confusing situations and making appropriate adjustments to connect with others of different cultures.

Let's go back to the example of eye contact. There's a tendency to confuse cultural preferences with personality traits. Could the person holding direct eye contact be perceived as rude and intimidating in Asian culture? Could the person consciously offering a fleeting glance be seen as untruthful or lacking confidence to an Australian?

Our cultural looking glasses are accustomed to our own societal rules and definitions of what is normal and what is not. When someone behaves differently to our own social codes, we can be quick to judge their behaviour as abnormal.

Recognising cultural expression as a learned behaviour separate from personality promotes a deeper level of understanding. Adapting to accommodate others' orientations fosters a rich connection. In the context of this book, it helps to think about your lens on culture helping you to understand yourself in relation to the different cultural groups around you.

Cultures are not static. Societies and communities are ever changing in response to social, economic, environmental and global shifts. Cultures are continually being renewed and reshaped.

Encountering another culture and respecting and accepting the similarities and differences from your own is a much-valued skill as our vast world shrinks into a global village. You cannot develop this level of empathy without sharpening your own self-awareness and recognising your personal cultural lens.

THE CULTURAL MIRROR

Can we be certain that we are not limiting our opinions of other cultures based on the visible traits – the tip of the iceberg – but rather delving deeper with curiosity to open the door on a rich cultural exchange? What if we could clear our filters and delete all preconceived ideas before we engage across cultural lines, to allow for non-biased engagement? To be open-minded and truly willing to connect, we need to hold up the mirror to our own cultural biases.

Diverse and divided

I arrived in the UAE in my early 20s. With a need to find a job, I noticed a strong recruitment drive as oil companies called out through adverts in the local newspapers for 'UK/US-educated secretaries'. I sped my way through secretarial courses, all with flying colours, to get the technical expertise on my résumé and spent the subsequent months getting in touch with recruitment agencies and responding to adverts directly.

My paper profile impressed recruiters enough that I made it to the first stage of phone interviews. However, excitement quickly gave way to disappointment when interviewers probed me on the origins of my name. Once they grasped that I was of Pakistani ethnicity, there was an awkward silence and the call was cut short. I never made it to the second round of interviews. I lost count of how many times this played out. It finally occurred to me that it wasn't about the UK/US qualifications – it was about the assumed UK/US white face.

Perhaps the hiring managers believed that I was less capable than a white candidate. As long as this assumption remained a thought, it was an unconscious bias. As soon as they acted on this idea, they crossed a line into another form of blatant bias that was prejudice. In this case, the belief that one candidate was superior to another solely based on ethnicity, more specifically the colour of their skin – that was racism.

The peril of unconscious bias is greatest when it seeps into all levels of society and becomes group thinking. Numerous studies have revealed that job candidates with foreign-sounding names have a significant disadvantage. In a test conducted by the BBC in 2017, Inside Out London sent CVs from two candidates, Adam and Mohamed, who had identical skills and experience, in response to 100 job opportunities. Adam was offered 12 interviews, while Mohamed was offered four. Although the results were based on a small sample size, they tally with the findings of previous academic studies.

A study out of Ryerson University and the University of Toronto came to a similar conclusion. According to a report published by the World Economic Forum in May 2017, as part of a different study from 2011, researchers sent out almost 13,000 fake résumés to over 3000 job postings. The academics went back to this data at the start of 2017 and found that people with Chinese, Indian or Pakistani-sounding names were 28 per cent less likely to get invited to an interview than the fictitious candidates with English-sounding names – even when their qualifications were the same.

We all hold unconscious biases, without even realising it. It is a natural human tendency. Think of a bias as a mental shortcut. It is a way of simplifying and categorising information in an attempt to make sense of the world around us. The brain defaults to stereotypes as a way of speeding up our social response in a complex social environment. Psychologist Mahzarin Banaji describes stereotyping as 'the unfortunate by-product of the otherwise immensely useful human ability to conceive the world in terms of categories'.

We make snap judgements about others all the time: in a restaurant, on the street, at a social event, when interviewing for a job. We rely on preconceptions to judge people from other groups. Stereotypes are beliefs that we have about broad characteristics of a group formed by our general knowledge or experience of that group.

Mental shortcuts

I would like to say that I am fully conscious of my own biases towards others, having dealt with my fair share of discrimination. That would only be partially true.

Born to first-generation Pakistani immigrant parents in the UK, I spent my formative years in Western society. My parents held the cultural values of their birth nation close, juxtaposing a counterculture of sorts to impart principles that I would not be exposed to in my immediate sphere. Even this did not prepare me for the four years I spent in Lahore, Pakistan, from the age of 19. I experienced culture shock, being expected to engage with a very different social attitude. I married my cousin within a year. Twelve years my senior, he was born and raised in Pakistan and associated more strongly with traditional Islamic culture.

Much later in life, I realised that my short experience in Pakistan had tainted my view of South Asians (a sub-region of Asia including the Indian subcontinent). It was not until I met my Sri Lankan-born, Hong Kong-raised partner, Wimal, that I was fully confronted with my own preconceptions.

In the early days of getting to know one another we visited a Pakistani restaurant for a late-night snack. I can't pinpoint what it was in that exact moment in that setting – the aromas, the music or the demeanour of the predominantly male clientele – that thrust me out of my comfort zone. Suddenly, seeing Wimal in that environment, alarm bells started sounding in my head. In a moment of inexplicable panic, I was ready to bolt.

The brain's flight-or-fight response reacts to social threats in exactly the same way it reacts to physical ones. My psychological defences had pieced together the image of a traditional life that I had escaped in Pakistan. In a fraction of a second, the man in front of me was about to become a casualty of my brain's hasty interpretation that he was somehow a threat.

Patriarchy is deeply embedded in Pakistani society. The social system is underpinned by Islamic and tribal influences in which men hold power over women. Placing constraints on the roles and activities of females, the traditional mindset dictates that women have their place – customarily, it is in the domestic sphere.

In contrast to my own personal experiences, women in Sri Lanka hold a higher position in society in comparison to other South Asian countries. In fact, in 1960, Sri Lanka was the first country in the world to elect a female prime minister.

Wimal grew up in the Christian faith, influenced by his highly educated family of doctors. He is more liberal than I am; comparatively I still have a conservative outlook. My subconscious mind had triggered strong emotions. In reality, the only feature that linked this man to my speculative fears of being dominated was the colour of his skin. I am embarrassed to say it, but it's true.

Being culturally diverse and having travelled extensively did not earn me a high score on the cultural intelligence index. I have been forced to hold up the mirror to my own biases, which admittedly were based on my thin-slice encounter of Pakistani society.

Clear thinking

Psychologist Daniel Kahneman outlines two systems of thinking in his book *Thinking, Fast and Slow*. System 1 is fast and intuitive. It is automatic and efficient. It seeks to quickly identify patterns, a skill that has been key to human survival but is also prone to mistakes. My System 1 thinking drove my impulse to run from the perceived threat embodied in a South-Asian male. System 1 thinking led me to draw rushed conclusions about his cultural beliefs.

System 2, on the other hand, is slow, deliberate and systematic. It seeks to test concepts and detect complexity and nuance. Kahneman suggests that System 2 articulates judgements and makes choices by endorsing or rationalising ideas and feelings that were generated by System 1.

So, how can we engage in clear thinking about intercultural incidents without retreating into psychological defences? Based on Kahneman's model, we can avoid jumping to conclusions on the instinctive and often sketchy interpretations resulting from System 1 thinking. We need to slow down long enough to question and rationalise our assumptions by consciously activating System 2 thinking. I managed to do this in the restaurant scenario – I didn't run, and was able to process what was playing out for me. I worked to identify the hooks that were keeping me in a habitual pattern of thinking and chose to delve beyond the apparent cues and uncover more about the person in front of me.

As I have learned, defaulting to mental shortcuts when making decisions about others can have serious negative ramifications. When we typecast people based on their observable culture, we put them in a box which in turn creates certain expectations about how they will behave. If we remain trapped in a habitual way of thinking and interacting with the world, we are disregarding exceptions to the generalisation. We are assuming things about people that may not be true.

THE CULTURAL PERSPECTIVE

When our perceptions of social groups shape our attitudes towards and feelings about people's character and abilities, we are crossing a line. Defaulting to a mental shortcut in judgement based on someone's name, gender or racial profile can deny them equal prospects. Is this fair?

Identifying bias

The story in chapter 2 highlighted racial prejudice. Gender and age are also subject to stereotyping and are prevalent themes of bias. Social norms and attitudes about the differences in men and women and what society deems appropriate behaviour for one sex over another breeds gender stereotyping.

As we will uncover in chapter 4, it is through multiple societal influences that children grow up identifying certain characteristics as belonging only to boys or girls. Gender discrimination is palpable in all spheres of life and manifests in life and career choices. Men and women tend to gravitate towards specific jobs because they are considered acceptable for their gender.

Different countries and cultures have different ideas about gender stereotypes, but we have all heard these statements: 'Men are insensitive.' 'He lacks emotional intelligence.' 'Women are better carers.' According to the Australian College of Nursing, registration data from 2017 showed that men make up less than 12 per cent of the registered nursing workforce in Australia. These figures are on par with comparable countries such as the UK, US and Canada where the proportion of men is similarly low.

Research conducted by Dr Vaughan Cruickshank at the University of Tasmania revealed that the number of male primary school teachers in Australia has been on a steady decline, dropping from 30 per cent in the 1980s to 18 per cent reported at the end of 2019. With the official statistics inclusive of principals, PE specialists and so on, Dr Cruickshank suggested the actual numbers in the classroom would be 15 per cent.

In part, Dr Cruickshank attributed the decline to social expectations to take on masculine or gendered roles. He said, 'Society needs to stop expecting male teachers to be the goal-kicking, football-coaching, tree-climbing, furniture-moving, father figure and all-round superhero'.

According to the Australian Government Workplace Gender Equality Agency:

> Multiple studies have demonstrated that when women
> apply for jobs, they receive fewer interview invitations
> than equally qualified men – an effect that is compounded
> for older women, women with children and women from
> certain ethnic or racial groups. Research has also shown

that men are similarly disadvantaged when applying
for entry-level roles or jobs in heavily female-dominated
occupations.

Generational stereotypes are just as real and dangerous. 'She's so entitled.' 'He's old school.' These labels are damaging, especially when false beliefs about a social category impact those people's chances of success. Does a sense of 'entitlement' mean a lack of commitment? Does being 'old school' mean someone will not master technological advancement? Ultimately these biases can tarnish someone's image. It is all too easy for prejudices to mutate into a 'them' and 'us' mentality creating a palpable cultural rift.

Think twice about your instinctive reactions. Do you have pre-conceived notions about people that are based on race, gender or age? You can recognise your biases by approaching different cultural groups and observing them without applying filters or trying to confirm predetermined ideas. What if you were to con-sciously 'blind' yourself from the individual's demographic and physical details when forming an opinion about them?

With conscious effort you can expand your self-awareness to reveal underlying prejudice. Within these pages lie ideas and new perspectives that can empower you to actively bust bias and arrive at a more complete and objective view of others.

Diverse and included

'Diversity' and 'inclusion' are big words in the business world today. Organisations are actively seeking to create a diverse workforce. More business leaders are getting behind diversity as it is definable and measurable, making it relatively simple to check off the strategy implementation list. There is an active drive to appoint more female directors to boards, the need to bring diversity of languages into customer-facing organisations, and an awakening to benefits of diversity of thought in leadership circles.

Inclusion, on the other hand, is not easily measurable. It is emotive; it is a feeling. US consultant Paolo Gaudiano sums it up perfectly when he states:

> We tend to notice inclusion only when we are feeling
> excluded, just as we tend to notice our health only when
> we are sick or injured. Inclusion is hard to measure directly
> because, in a way, it is invisible.

The words 'diversity' and 'inclusion' often appear together and start to merge in meaning; in reality, however, they are not interchangeable. Diversity is being invited to the party, while inclusion is being asked to dance.

Some years ago, many Australian businesses jumped on the bandwagon to recruit Mandarin speakers to capture the growing Chinese tourist spend. Significant marketing dollars were spent on understanding the Chinese buyer's mindset and targeting the tourist dollar through customised offerings. But how many business leaders actually invested time to understand the Chinese employee's mindset, and pave the way for inclusivity in the workplace?

Sophie, an Australian retail manager, is responsible for a team of customer service staff. Her boutique is located in a Chinese tourist hotspot in Melbourne, and her team comprises predominantly ethnic Chinese staff. One day, one of her team members was argumentatively justifying why his Chinese client should be offered a special discount. He suggested that Sophie 'needs to understand our culture'. Sophie felt confronted and somewhat disempowered as a middle manager. She later asked me, 'Who needs to understand who? We're in Australia; this is an Australian business'.

Part II of this book will shed light on some of the key differences between the Chinese and Australian cultures, among others, using a cultural values framework. It will give you many insights into how to bridge the differences rather than allow them to divide. For now, suffice to say that it is a two-way street, and that's exactly what I explained to Sophie to clear any traces of doubt. Both cultural groups must be strongly motivated to understand one another and work to bridge the cultural gap rather than stand ground on their own perspectives, which serves no-one.

In the case of Sophie's business, diversity was achieved in the active recruitment of a suitable mix of cultures. Leveraging that diversity involves giving each cultural group a voice. That's the starting point to cultivating an environment of inclusion. By initiating a dialogue that facilitates a better understanding of each other's cultural drivers we can make people feel heard and valued, starting the journey towards inclusion.

Busting bias

Many of the businesses I work with share a common threat: a lack of focus on integrating different cultures into their workplaces. Unless encouraged and motivated to do so, people are instinctively inclined to socialise with similar others. It is easier and more comfortable. This is known as affinity bias – the unconscious tendency to get along with others who are like us.

Team members socialise within their own cultural groups and revert back to speaking their mother tongue, especially where language is a potential barrier to engaging effectively with a larger group. A lot more effort is required to bridge differences in diverse environments.

Also known as ingroup bias, affinity bias is the tendency to favour our own social group more than groups of which we are not a member, referred to as outgroups. Studies show that people extend positive emotions and more trust, cooperation and empathy to ingroup members compared with outgroup members.

The group membership can become part of our identity. Communication across groups becomes more strained, and eventually there's a 'them' and 'us' at play as we start to see a silo mentality taking shape.

How does this play out in the workplace? If you work in a multicultural workplace, observe what happens at lunchtime. Cultural groupings will be more evident. Look for visual cues around social interactions. Are people of similar ethnicities drawing together? Are the groups based on age, gender, rank or language?

Favouritism towards groups you identify with can impact recruitment decisions, opportunities for promotion, who you chose to mentor, coach or support and who you chose to invite into your circle of trust. The group can be affiliated by cultural layers of gender or race, or similarities in socioeconomic status, fields of study or previous work experience. People in the outgroup feel excluded. This is counterproductive in achieving true inclusion.

Ultimately, learned perceptions have to be unlearned. Although the unconscious spark of bias is difficult to pinpoint, the plasticity of the human brain makes it possible to nudge our thinking through focused effort.

To heighten cross-cultural potential, we need to deepen our knowledge of other cultures and at all costs avoid relying on stereotypes. Being exposed to more culturally diverse environments with a spirit of openness will provoke new perceptions and expand cultural perspectives.

Be curious

Your circle of trust

Make a list of six people whom you trust most outside of your immediate family. Beside each name identify the following characteristics:

- gender
- age
- ethnicity
- nationality
- education
- faith
- sexual orientation
- native language
- professional background.

Looking at the list you have created, identify characteristics that are similar to your own. For example, if you are female, note how many of your trusted six people are female.

What does this show you about your trusted six? Does it highlight sameness or diversity? Which groups are not represented in your circle?

You can download a template for this exercise from the toolkit (please see details on page 141).

PART II
CULTURAL FILTERS

n part II of *Curious about Culture*, we explore the filters through which we view culture. As with any topic, there are many schools of thought and there are many models that offer perspectives on what shapes our personal culture. In this book, I will focus on the six perspectives shown in the figure below: gender, generation, faith, education, language and the national filter. As we define and demystify the six filters in this part, we will sharpen our understanding of ourselves and others.

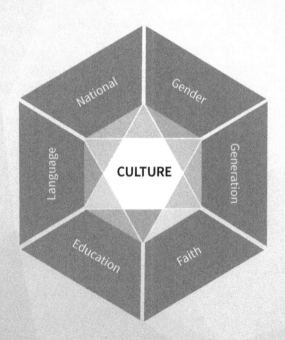

THE GENDER VIEW

Gender is one of the first social categories that we learn. Our birth certificates assign each of us one of two categories based on biological sex. From there we are exposed to ideas and expectations of how we should behave and express ourselves as we are gradually socialised into feminine and masculine roles.

Gender roles are socially constructed expectations that vary across cultures and within cultures. Looking to the model of cultural filters presented in the introduction to part II, we can start to visualise how several cultural filters such as faith, generation and nationality can overlay and reinforce ideas around gender. The influences of these social factors are augmented with messaging by parents, authority figures and even the media.

The traits of our assigned social categories, masculine and feminine, are often contrasted as 'tough and tender'. Femininity is predominantly associated with nurturing, caring and cultivating relationships. Masculinity is primarily associated with being assertive, goals-oriented and attaining material achievements.

Regardless of how individuals identify with their assigned gender, the danger is in assuming that all women solely embody feminine characteristics and all men innately, and only, possess masculine characteristics. We can each look to our own life experiences to affirm that we are continuously navigating the expectations of our social ecosystems. Circumstances often call for us to learn and unlearn, to negotiate and renegotiate imposed roles and their definitions as we grasp how best to show up in any given situation. I am certain that any single parent would agree that the experience of juggling the roles of nurturer, disciplinarian and breadwinner exemplifies the continuous metamorphosis of gender roles.

Identifying gender traits

Looking beyond the individual perspective, entities such as businesses, social groups and countries also have identifiable gender traits. The narrative of a nation is woven in the fabric of its society. In his well-known study of cultures, psychologist Dr Geert Hofstede highlights masculine/feminine leanings in national cultures and their impact on business. The cultural dimension of masculinity versus femininity considers societal preferences, attitudes and behaviours.

On the scale, Scandinavian countries such as Norway are considered highly feminine. Interpersonal attributes such as quality of life, physical environment and being of service are characteristic of feminine cultures. At a glance, we see evidence of gender parity in Norwegian political and business environments with equality represented across all tiers. Supportive policies and social welfare, including 12 months' parental leave after the birth of a child, and subsidised day care are also geared to ensure a level playing field.

At the other end of the spectrum, dominant values in masculine cultures revolve around success, money, rewards and possessions. In Japan, one of the most masculine societies in the world, these characteristics lie beneath a surface of collectivist cultural values and socially deferential behaviour. The Japanese are known to be workaholics, which challenges the ability of women to climb corporate ladders. In their drive for excellence and perfection, there's strong competition between groups, which is evident in business culture. My Japanese friend Hiroki tells of negotiations 'being simpler' back in the days when boys could fight it out in the playground. Borne of a feudal history and essentially cemented in school, that same battle is carried into the social fabric as corporate rivalry.

Recognising gender relations

Themes of gender are hotly debated across all layers of society today; gender equality is at the forefront of conversations in business, politics and at home. Underpinned by power structures, gender differences are undeniably subject to a hierarchy of value. Differences between genders are not neutrally distinguished; rather they are ranked and often become magnified.

As a consequence, gender hierarchies entitle one gender over another. Such hierarchy can be law enforced or entrenched in society as a result of underlying traditions. Regardless of the origin, the impact is the same: the empowered gender becomes dominant.

While the many voices that call for equality are becoming louder, inequality is still habitually ingrained in the collective mindsets of most societies and nations. As a result of generations of conditioning, suppressed genders timidly relinquish to power structures rather than attempting to contest them.

In most societies, men still dominate over women and are automatically awarded superiority. Examples of the reverse dynamic are so much harder to find. Delivering a speech on women and power, UN Secretary-General António Guterres reaffirmed that we have lived in a male-dominated world for millennia: a world that underpins our economies, our political systems and our corporations.

Saudi Arabia, a prime example, maintains patriarchal gender norms through repressive regimes against women. Females, by law, are subject to male guardianship; women require permission to study, travel, work and be married.

There are only a handful of societies in which women hold power and men are considered subordinate. According to National Geographic, the Mosuo tribe in China is said to be one of the last semi-matriarchal societies in the world, following a maternal bloodline and a structure that favours female agency.

Gender relational hierarchies exist in all tiers of our own personal ecosystems. Conditioning starts at home. Let's consider the hierarchy within a family. Does the father figure represent the steering factor or is femininity the ascendant driver? Do these dynamics inform our personal and professional relationships beyond the family unit? How do we carry these social paradigms into the external world?

The prevailing gender will differ across social groups. Compare this to an organisational culture that you manage, work for or interact with.

Not long ago, I visited a Tiffany & Co. boutique to purchase a graduation gift for my daughter. My partner accompanied me. We were greeted by a welcoming sales consultant who proudly showcased a selection of bracelets. The entire experience would have lasted around 45 minutes, during which time the consultant's attention was noticeably divided between my partner and me. He comfortably engaged with me in conversation related to Tiffany's design philosophy, varied options for engraving and the graduation event itself. All dialogue related to price, value for money and payment was markedly directed at my partner, whom he continued to refer to as 'your husband'.

Having spent a considerable part of my life in highly masculinised cultures, I didn't take offence. I could only hope that he might pick up on my repeated possessive expression towards *my* daughter rather than *our* daughter or finally learn something in retrospect after I concluded our shopping experience by presenting my own credit card. Was it that, through his own cultural conditioning, the sales assistant assumed a traditional family structure and thereby also assumed stereotypical gender roles – the man as the breadwinner? Or was his disposition tuned to a customer profile he encountered on a regular basis?

Organisations can be gendered, knowingly or unknowingly, in their practices and positioning – regardless of the gender balance in their workforce. If we elevate our thinking above the individual to the organisation, we could question whether the sales consultant was exhibiting learned behaviours of the business – perhaps it was the Tiffany way?

I encourage broader viewpoints that do not impose or rely on gender hierarchy when engaging with others. It is a precarious game of chance to make assumptions as to who the decision maker is and who controls the purse strings. It's a game that undermines roles and has potential to destabilise relationships. Inclusivity is key.

The gender spectrum

It often appears as though we are being asked to present ourselves as one or the other in regards to gender, with a demarcation as clear as black and white. In reality, we are adaptable to our environment and more often than not we are called upon to be more fluid in our roles.

Social and cultural norms influence the nature of interactions between genders. We are led to believe that women prioritise communication and tend to speak more openly than men, who rarely self-disclose in a bid to enact characteristics of confidence and strength. Is it clichéd? There are so many examples that contradict this idea in our everyday lives.

Consider a male friend who is less likely to divulge intimate details about himself or his loved ones with a group of masculine peers. The same friend is so much more likely to open up to a female friend in a one-on-one setting where he feels safe. The male gender is defined so rigidly that it can also trap men into stereotypes that require them to portray the macho image of powerful independence.

I can't think of a better way to bring the concept of gender dynamics to life than sharing a story about my personal passion: the dance of Argentine tango. There are expected norms in the tango community whereby a male leads the dance and a female follows, in what is essentially an improvised partner dance. As the *leader* and *follower* labels suggest, one role is more active and potentially more in control over the other role that can be viewed as passive.

In a modern-day world, many have broken with this tradition and created a subculture of sorts – one that equalises the power distribution. The newly adopted convention across some groups transitions a leader to a *proposer* who initiates a step. The traditional follower role then becomes the *interpreter* who decides how they wish to interpret the proposition and respond as if in dialogue. This allows either or both genders to step into either role with ease, at any time. As you might expect, the tango traditionalists reject – in some cases even prohibit – the idea of same-sex couples or ladies leading and men following in organised events. What if I told you that tango was born as a dance between male migrants who settled in Buenos Aires in the early 1900s?

I would like to provoke some reflection on how we show up on the feminine–masculine dimension in all our relationships with the external world, be they business, social or family interactions. Gender roles are learned behaviours. As with all cultural filters, views on gender are not static – they are interchangeable. The social rules governing what constitutes masculinity and femininity can also shift within a culture due to varying influences.

It is our obligation to broaden our viewpoints and remain open-minded about others' gender identities. Rather than intrinsically assigning roles to gender and taking a shortcut that enables biased notions, let's recognise where our own core beliefs influence how we view other gender cultures. Let's leave space for personal expression.

Be curious

Your cultural lens

- Can you identify the gender hierarchy within your family structure, your organisation and the social communities to which you belong?

- Picking up on social cues, we frequently adjust to our environments, dialling up or toning down our innate gender traits to respond to the prevalent culture. Where do you read and adjust to your environment? Where do you dial up or tone down your gender traits, either by choice or to fit in?

- Consider your professional self in a work setting. Think about your family dynamics and your social interactions. How are you seen? How do you want to be seen? How much freedom do you have to express your gender identity?

Curious about others

- In light of the gender hierarchy in your organisation and social groups, is one gender more entitled than another? How does this play out?

- Do these groups allow for freedom of gender expression or are members expected to fit into assigned roles?

- What needs to change for equality to become reality?

THE GENERATIONAL OUTLOOK

Looking through a generational lens offers a glimpse into another layer of personal culture: your own and that of others.

We have all experienced clashes at home as family members of different ages assert themselves to be right and challenge the wisdom of those who claim to know better. 'But you just don't understand.' 'How would you know?' Perhaps some of these everyday conflicts between grandparents, parents and teenagers sound familiar. To quote George Orwell, 'Each generation imagines itself to be more intelligent than the one that went before it, and wiser than the one that comes after it'.

Where were you when…?

Where were you at the start of the global financial crisis? Do you recall who you were with when the first plane hit the World Trade Center on September 11? Can you remember what you were doing when news of the Port Arthur massacre was first broadcast? What happened in your neighbourhood during the global pandemic of 2020?

Significant events such as these are known as generational defining moments. Chances are that you will remember one or more of these events vividly. If you experienced such an occasion in your formative years, somewhere between late childhood and early adulthood, it would have altered the world as you knew it and your personal beliefs in some way.

Of course, where you are at any given time and the impact of these events on you personally can vary greatly. I vividly recall the sombre mood as I followed the live broadcast of Princess Diana's funeral in 1997. I was living in Dubai and joined an estimated 2.5 billion viewers across the globe. At the time, it was the biggest-ever audience for a live television event under the modern system of measuring ratings. It was an emotionally charged event that I shared with fellow British citizens and so many other cultures across the world.

Earlier that same year, just 6000 kilometres to the east, my friend Amy witnessed the formal handover ceremony as the crown colony of Hong Kong officially reverted to Chinese sovereignty after more than 150 years of British rule. The British theme connected us, yet our experiences were vastly different based on our respective places of residence.

Collectively experienced moments shape perspectives and attitudes. Generational personality is influenced by economic circumstances, social changes and technological advancements. That's something you hold in common with others in your generational cohort.

Defining generational lines

There's some confusion around generational definitions. Lines can be blurred; start dates and end dates vary between sources. The references in this chapter are based on the categories defined by the Center for Generational Kinetics.

Generational bands are defined loosely by birth dates, not by age. A generation typically spans 25 years; think of it as a period of time between when someone is born to when they start having children of their own. Today you might think of Millennials as young adults aged, say, 25 to 33 years old. However, the term refers to a period of time in which members of the generation were born – in this case, between 1977 and 1995.

Generation Z

Born between 1996 and a date yet to be confirmed, this generation is also known as iGen, Centennials and Post-Millennials. As digitally connected citizens, Gen Z has a global perspective. Gen Z will graduate into a recession on account of the 2009 financial crisis and the global pandemic of 2020. These economic stressors will undermine this generation's ability to be independent and self-reliant. Gen Z were born into an era of increased gun violence, terrorism and war.

Generation Y

Born between 1977 and 1995, this group is more familiarly known as the Millennials, or the Internet Generation. They grew up amid a technology boom, effortlessly plugging into a world of social media, Google and video games. Millennials had early exposure to violent acts such as the Columbine and Port Arthur massacres, and were born into families that emphasised protection of their children. Environmental and social issues have been at the forefront of this generation's formative years; the *Human Rights (Sexual Conduct) Act 1994* formally legalised and liberated gay rights across Australia.

Generation X

Born between 1965 and 1976, Generation X was born into less traditional family structures than previous generations. Amid an era of dual-income households, higher divorce rates and single parents, they learned to become more self-reliant. This generation started to seek more work/life balance compared to previous generations. Influenced by the uncertainty of their times amid the stock market crash of 1987, Gen X saw terrorism at the Munich Olympics, the Lockerbie flight bombing and the fall of the Berlin Wall.

Baby Boomers

Born between 1946 and 1964, this band was coined the Baby Boomers due to the drastic rise in birth rates following the end of World War II. Baby Boomers were children of war veterans and peace movements. This generation started to question authority. People became more connected through the television, which broadcast impactful world news and events – from the assassinations of President John F Kennedy and Martin Luther King Jr to the first landing on the moon. The first nuclear power plant and the Civil Rights Act of 1964 were also definitive moments.

Silent Generation

Born in 1945 and before, this generation is also referred to as the Traditionalists. They were born in an era when people were not encouraged to speak openly about their views on current affairs.

Not surprisingly, then, this generation spurred the growth of the civil rights movement as key personalities challenged the status quo. Martin Luther King Jr, Fidel Castro, Malcolm X and Che Guevara were born to the Silent Generation. This group grew up amid extreme economic hardship between the Great Depression, World War II and the Cold War.

The multigenerational workplace

Generational diversity has great potential. People from different generations can learn from each other as they are exposed to one another's ideas and experiences. However, the potential for conflict and misunderstanding is also very real. With four generations in today's workplace, this cultural divide spills over into business. Here are some opposing schools of thought that can become a source of friction in the multigenerational workplace.

Work/life balance

The Baby Boomers lived the adage 'live to work'. They work hard and hold everyone else to account with a strong work ethic. Members of Gen X prefer the motto 'work to live'. Does this mean that one generation is more committed than the other? Boomers may be more visible at work, burning the midnight oil and clocking on and off; however, Gen X are just as engaged, even when they are not present at their desks. Advancements in technology mean that we can work from anywhere – from home or from a coffee shop. The 'work to live' motto fashions a work ethos around a lifestyle.

Millennials are equally vocal about wanting a life beyond work, and share Gen X's desire to achieve a work/life balance. Anecdotal observations suggest that Millennials are less disciplined than the older generations, who perhaps have a more structured approach to life in comparison. However, have you ever watched a Millennial balancing school assignments and social media chats with their headphones blaring full volume, only to ace their assessments with high distinctions? I have and, in my view, this generation epitomises successful multitasking.

Manage, lead or coach?

The younger generations are much less likely to take to authority and directive leadership in comparison to the Baby Boomers, who expect it.

Gen X are typically more self-reliant, dynamic and less likely to micromanage than previous generations. Gen Y generally respond better to a coaching leadership style than a directive one; they also want constructive feedback on how they can improve their skills. Shaped by an environment of instantaneity, Gen Z command immediate feedback.

Speaking about her predominantly Millennial team, a Gen X retail manager I worked with found that she had to recalibrate her expectations of her role to the realities of the increasing demands of her team. 'I find I'm constantly having to offer reassurance', she said. Baby Boomers and Gen X are used to waiting to be rewarded, and may find today that much more of their time is taken up with managing people.

Personal versus professional

The delineation of personal and professional in the workplace was clearer in previous generations compared to today, where the lines are increasingly blurred. Think back to when tighter internet policies were in place for employees before internet use became fundamental to business success. The use of social media in the office may have been a big no-no not so long ago, yet is a crucial tool today as businesses take to new channels to extend their reach. Sales teams stay connected with clients via Instagram, WhatsApp and WeChat on personal devices and reach out to personal networks to increase their business prospects. The rapid evolution of technology has changed the way people interact in business, with everyone becoming reachable at all hours.

Dress code is a good example of the distorted lines. Boomers and Gen X may be accustomed to suiting up for business engagements in a uniform-like professional attire. What was once suitable business wear in the traditional sense is no longer appealing to younger generations, who wish to express their identities more freely through a versatile desk-to-drinks style. I once worked with an HR professional responsible for more than 300 employees who found she had to cancel 'dress down Fridays' as the already casual code gave way to activewear deemed unsuitable for a workday. Many managers find it hard to enforce strict dress codes.

***

This is not to say that one preference is necessarily right and the other is wrong. Each generation's mindset is moulded by the social environment of the time. It is, however, about recognising the points of difference and facilitating an open dialogue to foster a deeper understanding across generations. By purposefully building bridges between the mindsets you can harness strengths across intergenerational communities.

The reality is that older generations will have to adapt to account for the different values of the changing workforce. As older workers retire from the workplace, the power in organisations is shifting to Generations X and Y.

It is time to start thinking about your generational outlook and how your cultural spectacles frame what you see.

Be curious

Your cultural lens

- Which generation do you primarily identify with? What are the specific characteristics of that generation?
- What is a generation-defining event that you experienced in your formative years? How may this have impacted your perspective?

Curious about others

- Which generation do you associate with or understand the least?
- How might this generation respond across the common themes identified in this chapter, and how is this similar or different to your own outlook? Consider:
  - work/life balance
  - manage, lead or coach
  - personal versus professional
- How can you learn more about the values of this group?

THE FILTER OF FAITH

Faith is most commonly interpreted as a religious belief system. I, however, think of faith as a religious or spiritual following. The filter of faith intends to be inclusive, and purposefully broadens the concept of culture in this context to respect the personal belief system of you, the reader.

There is a close relationship between faith and culture and an interplay between faith, culture and community. Community is essentially formed by a group of people who share common beliefs and activities. Belonging to a religious or spiritual group implies belonging to a particular culture. Faith is one of the many layers we explore as we disentangle our own cultural narratives.

One of the hallmarks of religion, of which there are many examples, is the organised structure that guides its members. The inner calling of spirituality connects people to a tribe of advocates, forming communality through practices such as meditation.

Ultimately faith-based philosophies define a social and moral code: what people expect of themselves and of others. These codes take form subliminally as guiding principles – call it that inner voice, your conscience or, as I will refer to later in this chapter, personal values.

Whether or not you are personally affiliated with a spiritual or religious system it is a cultural theme that influences people around you.

Faith may be regarded as a deeply private matter. While it can fundamentally represent the deepest form of connectedness, it can be one of the most subtly expressed tiers of culture. Not everyone will declare their personal belief systems – in some cases, for fear of animosity. Understanding this filter can, nevertheless, be profoundly eye-opening for those who profess to be curious.

Communities of faith

On the premise that culture is defined as beliefs, norms and values shared by a group, the lines between culture and faith start to blur. Faith shares a similar definition in addition to which practices, traditions, observances and rituals distinguish one denomination from another.

When we start to think of the rituals that socially connect people of a faith, we can see how it transpires into a cultural bond – a sense of belonging to an extended family. Religious institutions are widely known for creating a sense of community and a social support system for followers.

Communal worship is at the core of practising faith, be it in temples or in churches. Through words, music, dance or even silence, communities bond in collective worship. Congregational singing is one of the most social aspects of practice. Gospel choirs are legendary in Harlem churches; singing psalms is symbolic of the Jewish and Christian faiths. The dance of the whirling dervishes is a custom of Sufism. Festivities such as Easter, Hanukkah, Diwali and Eid mark highlights in community calendars.

These traditions become an integral part of life and a source of spiritual sustenance that can strengthen social bonds and a sense of community.

Cultural convergence or divergence?

Can you be Muslim and belong to Western culture? Can you be of Buddhist faith and belong to the Arabic culture?

Faith provides a source of identity, whether self-adopted or imposed by family or society. The strength of this filter ultimately depends on the degree of loyalty and devotion to a faith. If beliefs clash with national culture, members of a faith may be forced to practise cultural divergence to preserve their culture from external influence.

Culture can be divergent or convergent. While cultural convergence implies the coming together of cultures, cultural divergence is the reverse: one culture gives rise to different cultures. A combination of sociocultural factors in our respective communities will sculpt our individual experiences.

I have personally observed the vast difference in how Islam is practised in a predominantly Muslim country versus a nation that is home to a mix of beliefs and cultural influences. In short, I have seen varying levels of observance in cultural practices by different groups of followers.

As you might expect, it is harder to integrate traditional rituals into daily life where the individual's religious beliefs differ from the official national religion, thereby forging believers into minority groups. For a Muslim in a predominantly Christian society such as the UK, praying five times a day, fasting for 30 days or observing Friday as a sacred day go against social conventions.

On the other hand, in countries of origin, religion is embodied in a culture and an ethos of conformity is pronounced. In Pakistan, for instance, a conservative strain of religious beliefs is based upon inflexible interpretations of key teachings. Those who do not share these views and practices will feel more isolated.

The interpretations of the same religion were more relaxed among the expatriate community in the UAE. I noted how my friends and colleagues from the Levant[1] adopted a more lenient approach, selecting practices befitting a desired cultural lifestyle. Typically, they were fasting during Ramadan, abstaining from alcohol (only during Ramadan) and forgoing the five daily prayers. The breaking of the fast at sundown was a celebrated affair bonding friends and family.

Social codes in a community bound by faith

The social codes of the Mormon faith are more consistent the world over. Local churches teach the same lessons, practise the same principles and adopt the same values. The unified culture of Mormonism is discernible as newcomers are embraced by peers in churches everywhere in the world from Malaysia to Japan to the US to New Zealand.

---

1   The Levant denotes a geographical region situated in the Eastern Mediterranean, roughly from Greece to Egypt. The countries that comprise the Levant are characterised by similar linguistic, cultural and religious traits and include Syria, Lebanon, Turkey, Jordan and Palestine, among other nations.

As those who practise Mormon faith will endorse, the real story of the Mormons is the success of community, upheld by the church to be 'rooted in both self-reliance and communitarian idealism'.

In a coaching conversation, my client, John, recollected his summer job at a local bakery in a rural town in the north island of New Zealand during his impressionable young teens. Proud of his new earnings, he invested in a staggeringly heavy sack of wheat as a Christmas gift to his family. A far cry from the commercial images of Christmas gifting, adding to the family food storage for use in case of flood, unemployment or unforeseen disaster was predicated on Mormon principles of self-reliance and contribution.

John's pious filter of faith was shaped by his parents, his seven siblings, his church and his community. Underlying the philosophy of any religion are mutual values that govern and shape the observer. These values predominantly define how members behave and interact with one another and the world at large. These teachings at a very early age were ingrained as part of Mormon culture and had a strong bearing on John's personal values as he transitioned to adulthood.

Four decades into his life, as divorce and subsequent separation from his family coincided with the loss of his job, John's sense of self was deeply shaken. Mormon culture focuses on the family unit, and activities and teachings revolve around family, so as a divorcee he found himself on the outside of the community with less to contribute, identify with and belong to.

Religion and spirituality are often deeply tied to identity. Arriving at a junction where you find yourself no longer in alignment with a system of faith, for whatever reason, can lead to strained relationships with the very community that defined your sense of being. Worse still, it can lead to being ostracised and excluded.

Forced into a deeply introspective phase in life, John started to question his long-held beliefs and recognise what might be preventing him from living a fully expressed life. This forged a deeper exploration of his personal values at a more profound level.

Through a series of conversations, we uncovered a theme of underlying values instilled in his childhood from the Mormon faith. A desire to be of service to fellow beings, belong to a community and find financial freedom were all important characteristics of his religious studies. Realigning to these values for a full expression of the same involved identification with new communities – socially and professionally.

How faith shapes personal values

As a coach, unpacking John's personal life experience in the context of religious influences and bringing his core values to the forefront was an enriching experience to witness. His journey, however, is not unique. Through in-depth coaching conversations with leaders in religious communities, I have observed individuals – a former elder of the Jehovah's Witnesses and a pastor of the Hillsong Church – who went to great pains to disassociate from the confines of religious boundaries despite deep respect for their core philosophies. Unequivocally, this was to the greater disappointment of their respective families and communities, where common values were shared by groups.

In both of these cases, the individuals' seniority and appreciation of responsibility towards others were ingrained in the very fabric of their being. Their innate sense of obligation to the community and their desire to belong, contribute, teach and guide did not dissolve. The paradigm merely shapeshifted into non-religious, personal cultural values.

The beliefs that we hold and the values that we embody are essential parts of our identity. Ultimately, they govern our experiences; they reflect who we are and how we live our lives. Values have a significant influence on most of the judgements we make as well as persuading the support we offer to others.

As each of our personal cultural narratives is unique, each one of us is entitled to our own values, attitudes and beliefs. Where these differ, we can meet one another at the borders of cultural identity with curiosity, understanding and respect.

Be curious

Your cultural lens

- Do you associate with a religious, spiritual or philosophical belief system?

- If so, how does this affiliation shape your view of the world?

- What values might your faith have encouraged?

Curious about others

- Do you know the religious, spiritual or philosophical belief systems of those in your immediate circle such as your extended family, friends and colleagues?

- Does their affiliation contribute to, or broaden, your view of the world?

- Does your organisation accommodate employees' practices of faith and recognise variances in value systems?

THE EDUCATIONAL LENS

Education reflects the social, political and cultural patterns of society. Combined, these factors shape our lens on the world. What we are taught and how we are taught it greatly influences our ideas and how we express them through life.

As you look to your own personal experiences, you might recognise that your educational journey started at home. Early schooling teaches social skills and behavioural patterns for a world within and beyond the playground, as we are groomed to become members – or rather good citizens – of a larger society. Moulding the outlook of tender young minds, education transmits knowledge and skills as well as ideas to new generations.

The journey of learning

As you reached for this book, you demonstrated a thirst for knowledge. We are in fact lifelong learners: our education does not begin or end in school or university. Informal education exists outside the walls of classrooms through community and activity-based programs, from museums and libraries to self-learning approaches.

Formal education is commonly classroom based, structured via a curriculum and facilitated by professional teachers and trainers. In some cultures, senior family members play an integral role in imparting knowledge to strengthen, or sometimes even substitute, the formal education system.

Across cultures, tutoring styles may combine multiple approaches or rely on one main methodology. These approaches are guided by the social and cultural determinants in a specific school, institute, organisation, country or even region.

Different teaching tactics will stimulate varied learning attitudes: from a directive delivery style that promotes learning through listening and following directions; an interactive approach that promotes learning through lively discussion; to a socially inclined system of group work and peer feedback.

Each of these teaching methodologies fosters a wide spectrum of skills such as critical thinking, empowerment and collaboration. They also assign varying levels of expectations and assumed responsibility between the teacher's role to educate and the recipient's role to learn. Ultimately, learners of all ages are products of nature and nurture; our innate personality combined with our learned cultural traits ultimately shape how we learn.

My friend Eva, an academic professional, tells me that the German language has a metaphor that presents a new way of looking at our learning journeys. *Bildungsbiographie* literally translates as 'education biography'. The term was popularised in modern-day multicultural Germany to recognise the different educational pathways of students who, at some juncture, join the

German education system. The concept acknowledges the right to access education despite varied educational histories. Individual learning pathways are intersected by choices, opportunities and circumstances. Acknowledging diversity within the population, an educational biography details the student's unique history – similar to a résumé that captures work history.

Learning cultures in the workplace

With the knowledge that culture influences how people learn and teach, businesses cannot bypass the fact that multicultural teams call for a combination of approaches to the creation of learning experiences.

Sam, a Training and Development Manager at the Australian office of a large German business, called me with grave concerns about the suitability of a leadership training program imposed upon her management team in Australia. The program was designed by her organisation's regional headquarters in Singapore for rollout across the Asia-Pacific region. After an 'immensely successful' pilot launch in Singapore, a trainer had been appointed to lead the delivery in Australia. The dates were set and booked.

During Sam's few interactions with the trainer, she had developed a hunch that the trainer's unexpectedly standoffish communication style was not going to suit his management group. Relatively new to her job, Sam felt responsible for the delivery of the program. Anticipating a less-than-smooth experience ahead, she asked me to sit in on the training session and provide independent and objective feedback on the content and facilitation.

Training day arrived. After a few quick introductions and an overview of the agenda, the program commenced. A barrage of narrated slides was occasionally interjected with a question from the team. Visibly awkward, the facilitator deflected the actual questions and continued to 'talk at' his audience.

It was apparent that one quarter of the room was attentive while the rest of the group was twitching between eye rolls and restless fingers reaching out for devices to entertain themselves. I was struggling to stay focused as the words 'death by PowerPoint' echoed in my mind.

The oversight here was that decision-makers assumed the regional training needs could be addressed by one program with a singular approach. The Asia-Pacific region comprises a diverse set of cultures, from India to New Zealand and Japan to Fiji. Was it fair to assume that each culture would relate to the content and delivery with the same level of ease as the Singapore team?

The influence of culture on learning styles

Earlier, I touched upon educational systems that differ in terms of their teaching style, delivery method and student expectations. Different cultures have varied approaches to learning. Numerous studies on this topic highlight that approaches to teaching and learning in Western and Eastern educational systems are fundamentally different. I should interject here to explain that I am not entirely comfortable with the broad definitions of East and West. Is Australia in the West? It's down to perspective, and it could be argued that it depends which map you are looking at. While Australia has its European roots in the cultural and economic West, geographically it is about as far away from the West as one could get. However, in this instance the simplification provides us with a straightforward approach to illustrate some general differences and stimulate thought.

Based on this classification, let's look to the East. In countries such as China, Japan and India, the emphasis is traditionally on conformity with rules and regulations that students are expected to follow. Lectures are the main mode of instruction, with the teaching method being predominantly a one-way direction. As a consequence, memorising and retaining information is the goal, with a focus on examination results and grades. Formality prevails in these cultures: teachers are revered and seen as authoritarian. The method commonly associated with learning in these parts of the world is known as 'rote learning' – a technique based on memorisation and repetition.

In Singapore, students rely on rote learning and extra tuition to get through exams. This is believed to be driven by the Singaporean concept of *kiasuism* – in Hokkien, a Chinese dialect, it means 'afraid to lose'. A desire for continual betterment through strong academic results is entrenched in the collective mindset.

On the contrary, a teacher acts as a facilitator in Western education systems (in this case we are looking to the Australian and German cultures). Open discussions, debates and sharing of ideas are encouraged in the classroom, offering a sense of ownership to the learning experience. These systems encourage individual talent, creativity, assertiveness and critical thinking.

We know that culture and learning are connected, but it would be unreasonable to assume that each learner is a product only of their learning environment. Let's also be aware that many people pursue further education opportunities abroad, so their learning experiences are further nuanced through a combination of styles. It would be more beneficial to understand the expectations of the learning process from the learner's perspective which is fundamental to the instructional design of workplace learning.

Going back to our case study, the Asia-Pacific training program failed to engage everyone effectively. It was a one-way methodology of telling rather than open discussion and discovery to suit the diversity in the room. It also represented a missed opportunity to provide broader context and deeper relevance to the leadership team. The investment in a regional training program is considerable. Failure to deliver on learning objectives due to cultural differences is a costly oversight.

There are some fundamental considerations when planning learning and development programs for multicultural groups. Awareness around cultural influences on learning styles is important in enabling the transfer of skills and knowledge. Those responsible need to consider how to create a learning culture that exposes all participants to multiple perspectives and connects them with alternative views of the world.

One of the most advantageous aspects of working in a cross-cultural team is the diversity of ideas and approaches to learning that it brings. Participants can learn so much from one another when diversity is acknowledged and given space to flourish.

Be curious

Your cultural lens

- If you were to write up a brief education biography for yourself, what would it suggest about your learning journey?

- How has your educational pathway shaped the way you learn? How would you describe your preferred learning style?

- What is your expectation of a teacher or trainer? How much responsibility do you assume for your own learning?

Curious about others

- What is your observation of the learning culture of your organisation? Does your organisation cater to different learning styles?

- If you are in a teaching, coaching or mentoring role, consider the learner's preference versus your own. Are there similarities or differences?

- Are there ways in which your organisation could bridge the gap between different teaching and learning styles?

THE LANGUAGE CODE

Culture and language reciprocally influence each other. Language is fundamental to cultural identity and unifies people of the same cultural group. The English language is one cultural identifier that unites you, the reader, with me, the author.

English has expanded beyond the border of England to become the official language of multiple nations, from Canada to New Zealand. For those of us who speak English as a first language there is comfort in knowing that it is widely accepted as an international language, however it does not have the highest number of native speakers. Mandarin and Spanish far exceed native speakers while English is followed by Hindi and Arabic as fast-growing language communities.

It is believed that language shapes how we think. Lera Boroditsky, psychology professor at Stanford, says that the languages we speak not only reflect or express our thoughts, but also shape the very thoughts we wish to express. How we make sense of the world is shaped by inferences in language. Ultimately, we extrapolate meaning from language.

Imagine then the complexity in communication across different languages. For those who speak English as a second or foreign language, expression of thoughts and ideas may be inhibited by the confines of a borrowed vocabulary.

To truly appreciate the essence of a culture you would need to grasp the language that offers a window into its traditions and beliefs. As Nelson Mandela famously stated, 'If you talk to a man in a language he understands, that goes to his head. If you talk to him in his own language, that goes to his heart.'

Culture is ingrained in language

Language has important social functions. We use language to convey cultural beliefs and norms, and it is encrypted with cultural values.

Some languages reflect layers of formality by simply applying a more formal or informal tone. Others rely on specific grammar to distinguish differences, depending on the social situation. In English, the word 'you' serves as a second-person pronoun in both singular and plural forms. The French language, as an example among many, allows for a distinction between formality *(vous)* and informality *(tu)*. The pronoun indicates a relationship to the person being addressed. These formal and informal customs of how people are addressed denote esteem for seniority, be it in age, rank or relationship. The language of culture caters to conveyance of societal respect for status and a range of vocabulary allows for suitable expression.

The meaning of a message is not restricted to words alone. As we decode a language, we must appreciate that tone, too, plays a big role.

My client, Firdous, was baffled by an exchange with her colleague. She politely asked, 'Can you print 10 copies of this document?' He strenuously retorted with, 'Please!'. Was her colleague teaching her to speak English? Was he implying that she was rude? New to Australia, Firdous speaks English fluently even though it is her second language. The word 'please' does not exist in her mother tongue – Hindi. In fact, it does not exist in many languages, including Arabic, Urdu and Farsi. A polite request is suggested through the intonation of 'can you'. However, for a native English speaker, if the request is not supplemented with the word 'please' it appears imbalanced and disrespectful.

Patterns in language offer a window into the nuances of a culture. Beyond an assortment of words, language also preserves cultural heritage. Humility is an underlying concept in Japanese culture, one that is shown through customs of bowing and expression of gratitude but also in politeness of speech. Unlike most Western languages, the Japanese language has extensive grammar to convey politeness and formality. Reflecting the values embedded in Japanese society, *aisatsu* offers numerous forms of greetings which simply translate to 'hello' or 'goodbye' in the English language. There is an appropriate *aisatsu* for each cultural group and setting corresponding to the hierarchical structure of society.

If you speak a Romance language – one that originates from Latin, such as Spanish, Portuguese, Italian and French – you will know that gender appears in almost every phrase through feminine and masculine words and articles. The genders of adjectives correspond to their accompanying nouns such as in the Spanish examples *la bahia blanca*, the white bay (f) or *el mar blanco*, the white sea (m). While researchers continue to decipher whether gendered languages influence the way native speakers think, it has been determined that gender association to inanimate objects is stronger. A Spanish speaker is likely to attribute masculine characteristics to the sea (bold, rough) compared to feminine traits of a bay (calm, beautiful).

Decoding language

While language is a dominant force that unifies English-speaking countries there are perceptible differences and distinct personalities across the national cultures.

Aside from the obvious differences in accent, pitch and minor grammatical variations, the English dialects are separated by underlying codes of culture. British, Australian and American cultures share relatively direct communication styles, as is revealed in more detail in part III of this book. Nonetheless, Brits tend to obscure direct confrontation under statements such as 'that's interesting' or 'with all due respect' as a prelude to disagreement, whereas Australians and Americans tend to be more forthright.

According to linguistics expert and author Edwin Battistella, English speakers use the word 'sorry' in different ways. Brits say 'sorry' more often, but this doesn't necessarily mean that they are more remorseful. British society values that its members show respect without imposing on someone else's personal space, and without drawing attention to themselves – characteristics that linguists refer to as 'negative-politeness'. Apologising for other people's mistakes and even things out of the speaker's immediate control such as the weather pushes Brits to use the word more casually. As a consequence, 'sorry' features excessively in day-to-day language.

In contrast to British English, Australian English leans towards informality; Australians opt to shorten words wherever possible. As a native English speaker, I recall having to defer to colleagues for translation in my efforts to decode Aussie English – even in business settings – during my early days in the country.

To the uninitiated, cross-cultural interpretations of concepts in language can create an obstacle course in themselves.

While on the phone one day with my South African colleague, Jan, we agreed to meet for an impromptu drink that same evening. Before ending the call, Jan suggested that he pick me up en route. 'I'll see you just now', he said. Expecting him to arrive at any moment, I rushed to get ready and then I waited … and I waited. He sent an SMS almost an hour later to tell me that he was now on his way and expected to reach me in 10 minutes. By this point I was beginning to feel agitated, but also confused. Jan was one of the most punctual and disciplined people I knew: always on time to work and for meetings, if not early. I let it go in favour of a peaceful evening; after all, perhaps I had misunderstood. A few days later I called Jan for a business matter; he suggested he was busy and would call me back 'just now'. Again, assuming 'just now' meant 'any minute', I stayed by the phone waiting for it to ring. Forty-five minutes later Jan returned my call. At this point I was sure it was not my mistake! As I confronted him about his tardiness he started to laugh, much to my annoyance. Then he explained that 'just now' doesn't actually mean 'now', it means 'in a bit' or 'sometime in the very near future'. In my book, 'now' means 'right now', yet the cross-cultural interpretation of one English word was so different.

When social vocabulary becomes mainstream

The language differences across national lingual borders are both discernible and expected. It is the invisible borders across organisational, societal and community language that can catch us unaware. I alluded to these borders when I shared my brief cross-cultural encounter in the introduction. We are continuously navigating cultural borderlines across gender, generation and national identities.

As the English language evolves, our vocabulary too increases. Several hundred words are added to the *Oxford English Dictionary* annually. The following examples demonstrate new additions that speak to the inclusion of social language, used by groups based on gender, occupation and age, into a mainstream lexicon.

'LOL', to laugh out loud, is less likely to be adopted by older generations with the ease with which a tech-savvy generation coined it for purposes of compressing language across the wires. The act of explaining became gender-specific as 'mansplaining' came into being – perhaps a term more frequently used by females when referring to men. There are differences in language used between, say, a university professor and a corporate employee. MBI – management buy-in – is a term that's likely to be used in an organisational context among work colleagues. With the advent of the gig economy comes more vernacular distinctive to peer groups. The term 'gig' today commonly describes jobs that last a specified period of time and is used by freelancers and independent contractors, but was derived from popular musicians referring to their specific engagements.

Some lingo does not translate effectively across social groups, industries and generations. This calls for explanations to avoid excluding people and powering the ingroups that we discussed in chapter 3.

***

Communication across cultural groups is laden with complexity. On a daily basis we communicate across generations, genders, nationalities and so on. Complications arise when we impose our own cultural standards to delineate what is right, what is wrong, what is acceptable and what is not. Misunderstandings are rife in rushed exchanges where one or both parties jump to hasty conclusions. Communication is a two-way street between the speaker and the listener. It remains a joint responsibility to then understand the cultural context in which communication transpires.

Be curious

Your cultural lens

- What presents the biggest communication challenge in your workplace and can you identify the reason?

- How does this influence your ability to get your intended message across in the different cultural groups with whom you interact?

- How might you be able to adjust your communication style to avoid confusion?

Curious about others

- Looking to the groups with whom you regularly interact, what languages, native to others, are in the mix?

- How does this influence the ability of others to get their message across?

- What allowances can you make for differences in language and how you interpret the messages of others?

9

THE NATIONAL DIMENSION

The dimension of national culture is an integral facet in defining our personal culture, however I have been intentional in leaving this filter to the end of part II. As we peel back this last layer, we have already systematically revealed that we are products of an assortment of influences from our respective social ecosystems. We have established that personal culture is intersected by multiple factors such as gender, generation and faith. It is my hope that this idea is firmly planted in your mind space as there is a natural tendency to resort to cultural similarities and differences based on perceptions around nationality.

Let's pause in this moment to reflect on the meaning of national culture. Is it part of our identity? Do we associate with a national culture that prescribes 'the way we do things here'? What do you think of when you think of national identity? A passport, a border, a language or a national hero, perhaps? Nationality is merely a legal status of citizenship but not an accurate personal identifier as such. Ethnicity runs deeper to encompass everything from language to racial identity, ancestry and religion to better reveal our cultural identities. Throughout this book I have described myself as British-Asian living in Sydney, Australia. I did not merely identify myself based on my citizenship, my town of birth or my place of residence, which I believe to be a limiting self-description.

To rely heavily on national culture alone forms a myopic view and leads us to the trap of stereotyping, which does not accurately reflect cultural identities or predict beliefs or behaviour.

Is national culture bound by geographic borders?

Globalisation, migration and sociopolitical changes all contribute to the evolution of national cultures. Added to this, more progressive views of younger generations broaden perspectives and loosen the grip on long-established traditions.

We can be tempted to associate national culture within geographic borders. It is, of course, so much easier to default to ideas that support our preconceived beliefs – 'Well, she's American, therefore …' There may be qualities and values that most Americans commonly share, however we cannot assume that all Americans think or act the same way.

Although the US is primarily identified as a Western culture, its vast size and history of immigration has formed subcultures. US-based journalist and author Colin Woodard distinguishes between 11 regional cultures that embody the nation. Take, for example, El Norte, which includes parts of Texas, Arizona, New Mexico and California. Hispanic culture dominates in the area, and the region values independence, self-sufficiency and hard work above all else. Compare this to the West Coast where people are known for their love of the outdoors and their care for the environment; life is a bit slower, with priority given to happiness and personal endeavours over career success and achievement. The Northeast region, home to some of the largest US cities like New York, Boston, Philadelphia and the capital Washington D.C., is largely industrialised and life there is fast paced.

Some societies diverged in the course of history. We can look to Africa's Rainbow nation as home to a spectrum of cultural identities that are being reclaimed and defended in post-apartheid South Africa, in exchange for a cohesive cultural identity across its multicultural landscape. Divided by heritage, race, language, religion and tribe, South Africa is a rich tapestry of distinctly different cultures contained within the borders of one nation.

Geographically we may see Hong Kong as a part of China, though it has a unique history that has shaped a hybrid culture differentiated from that of the mainland. As a British colony, Hong Kong society evolved quite differently with a democratic system of local government, free press and a culture that was deeply influenced by British laws and sensibilities.

The world around us is changing rapidly. The paradigms that define national cultures are evolving. We need to remain cognisant and open-minded about how individuals and societies are disarranged around these migratory and social shifts.

The need to belong

When we think of migration it conjures the idea of opportunity – a change for the better. Environmental, socioeconomic and educational factors are just some of the possible motivations to migrate to a different state, country or continent. Relocation, however, is not always voluntary. There are those who are forced to flee from their homes for a number of reasons that talk to personal safety. When people move away from their family structures, social groups and religious communities they lose an inherent part of their identity. Whether forced or not, when someone is placed in a new culture, they have to adapt to it as a means to belong.

The national dimension provokes one of the strongest associations of belonging. Some migrants flock towards a comfortable bubble of their own cultural community for reasons of shared language and cultural customs. Points of commonality forge acceptance and the security of a more immediate support network. Some migrants absorb the prevailing culture in order to adjust to their new environment while retaining elements of their original cultural heritage. Others add more diversity in their new nations making tangible contributions. We have all tasted cultural expression through culinary mashups that originate from these permeating fringe culture groups. Migrant Japanese married their culinary techniques with Peruvian ingredients to give birth to Nikkei cuisine. Indian curries are not only a staple menu item in British pubs, but British Indian curries feature as a national dish in the UK.

As social beings, we have an intrinsic need to belong to social groups. People often present themselves in a particular way as a means to belong. One of my business associates, Hooman, tells stories of his growing years as his family migrated from Iran to Canada to Dubai before finally settling in Australia. 'Football was my segue to social acceptance', he says. 'I just knew I had to be good at the game so that no-one would question where I was from.' Sporting activities, however competitive, unite people and welcome outsiders into the fold based on their skill level.

Hooman's astute observation of football as a shared connection won him friendships that then went beyond the playing field and transpired into meaningful connections in his newly adopted home country.

It is not simply a case of unpacking a suitcase and presenting a passport as a plane touches down in a new country – there is so much more to unpack in a newly adopted homeland. There is also so much that gets left behind. Global movement invites a diverse cross-section of the world to live and work together. Categorising one another into predefined cultural boxes is limiting at best and damaging at its worst.

'Where are you from?'

Imagine you are at a social party or a work event surrounded by new people. In conversation, you find yourself curious about someone's cultural background. You might be tempted to ask, 'where are you from?' Even if you mean well, for those on the receiving end, the question may have deeper implications than you may realise.

I arrived in Dubai in the early 1990s with an impressionable one-year-old daughter. The cultural melting pot was our home for 18 years. That was a lifetime compared to the many expatriates who came and went on shorter-term contracts. Zehra was raised and schooled in the emirate. As far as she knew, it was home.

As much as she identified with being 'from Dubai', she wasn't entitled to own the label. We knew that we were without status in the UAE. Unlike Australia, which offers a pathway to permanent residency, life in the UAE was punctuated at four-year intervals as employment visas came up for renewal.

Zehra was raised in Dubai, visibly of South-Asian descent, holder of a British passport, with a British-Asian mother and a Pakistani father – 'where are you from?' is not an easy question for her to answer. It was no wonder, then, that a seemingly benign question could literally shake Zehra's world. The question was a default conversation starter in Dubai and a fair line of enquiry given that at any single point in time the local Emiratis barely made up a fifth of the total population. Everyone else was 'from' somewhere.

It was a constant source of grief for Zehra as she grappled with her sense of identity and belonging until, thankfully, she stumbled upon an article that awarded her a status: a 'third culture' kid. Well into her teens by this point, she now belonged to a cool new generation of kids. The term was coined decades ago to describe those who spend their formative years in places that are not their parents' homeland, and is gaining more importance in today's era of globalisation. As sociologist Ruth Van Reken warns, life as a third culture kid can create a sense of rootlessness and restlessness, where home is 'everywhere and nowhere'.

At the face of it, seeking to know where someone is from is merely a way of building a connection. In most cases, however, it is also loaded with presumptions. As Zehra can tell you, she would like to say that she is 'from Dubai', but she can't. 'If I say I'm British, I get puzzled looks – clearly I don't look British, so that doesn't satisfy people.' Then comes the interrogation – 'But where are you *really* from?' Zehra says, 'I then feel I have to fill that awkward moment of silence by going on to explain my cultural identity. By this point, any motivation to build a connection is lost'.

Intercultural relationships are giving birth to more and more third culture kids. Nationality alone is not a cultural determinant and those who rely on this classification only are depriving themselves of a potentially rich interpersonal exchange.

Be curious

Your cultural lens

- What is your nationality and what does nationality mean to you?
- Does your nationality reflect your cultural identity?
- If so, how? If not, why not?

Curious about others

- How many people in your direct circle identify with their national status?
- Would your friends or co-workers be comfortable being asked, or answering the question, 'where are you from?'
- Why is that?

PART III
CULTURAL VALUE DIMENSIONS

Our basic cultural values are acquired from our social environment. We adopt the dominant values from our families, peers, communities and society at large. Studies suggest that we do this during the first 10 years of our lives. As these values are learned implicitly at a formative stage, they continue to act as a subconscious guide, directing our behaviour through life.

If I ask you to define your cultural values, you might struggle to respond specifically to such a broad question. However, if I ask 'what is your definition of success?' perhaps you could define it as status, freedom or individual achievement. Or perhaps, for you, it means contributing to community growth and wellbeing.

What if I pose the question, 'what does it mean to be a good citizen?' You may believe that it is to express and support others in voicing their opinions and asserting freedom of individual rights. Alternatively, you might say that it is to respect those in authority and defer to decision-makers as per the expectations of society at large.

These questions would shed light on your beliefs around identity in relation to groups and your relationship with authority respectively. Framing these questions around a model will guide you to reflect and respond more deliberately.

In part III of *Curious about Culture*, I introduce a framework of cultural value dimensions. As a certified professional with the Cultural Intelligence Center (CQ Center) I am using their validated model. In each of the following six chapters, we will explore the six value dimensions which have the greatest potential for confusion and misinterpretation in personal and professional life.

For context, the cultural values we explore here are the core principles and ideals upon which an entire community or society exists. In this case we look at typical orientations across 10 geographical clusters, which are listed in the table on page 82.

Interpreting the cultural value dimensions

Each of the six cultural value dimensions distinguishes between two orientations on a scale. For instance, when we unpack the 'identity' value, we will look to a scale that plots *individualism* – emphasis on individual goals and rights – on one side versus *collectivism* – emphasis on group goals and personal relationships – on the other. These are not black-and-white oppositions; each geographical cluster sits somewhere between the two polar opposites, but does not necessarily represent an extreme. Your personal preference will also sit somewhere on the continuum.

The intention of introducing this framework is to direct your awareness to your default orientation. With the reminder that *Curious about Culture* aims to be introspective, the values will primarily promote a deeper understanding of why you may be motivated to act differently to other people.

Opaque differences in cultural values, across geographical boundaries or within domestic borders, can lead to misunderstandings and a clash of cultures. Bringing these variances to the forefront creates opportunities to build bridges and helps you to address these gaps. The intention is not to create social division through over-generalising about someone based on their association with a particular geographic group.

Going deeper, you can consider your preferences in relation to those of others and learn to decode the others' behaviours. An understanding of how these values play out can prevent you from incorrectly attributing someone's behaviour to their innate disposition and capabilities.

A set of 'Be curious' questions presented at the end of each value chapter will help you to uncover your preferences and offer insights to power your interactions with people of different cultural orientations.

Part III of *Curious about Culture* provides you with judgement-free vocabulary to start an exploratory dialogue and gain useful perceptions across perceived cultural borders.

As we delve into the cultural value dimensions one at a time, it is important that I highlight a few considerations:

- Your values, and those of others, just are; they are not right or wrong. There is no better or worse along the continuum. Our preferences influence how we show up and engage with the world around us.

- Cultural values tend to remain stable over time and they may influence your personal interests and career choices.

- The model is provided for self-reflection and relies entirely on your self-awareness. If you would like to uncover, more precisely, your orientation against these cultural values, you can choose to do a cultural values profile. The concluding chapter, 'Want to know more?', provides further detail on this.

Global clusters and their orientation

At the end of each cultural value you will find a reference to global clusters positioned along the continuum. These clusters represent typical cultural value preferences for the 10 largest cultural groupings in the world. Our individual perceptions may reflect our national or cultural groupings; then again, they may not.

Understanding typical cultural values in the different clusters provides an initial starting point for thinking about variances that might be encountered in that cultural cluster. Comparison of personal cultural value preferences with typical preferences for specific cultural clusters provides an indication of variances that may be encountered with people who identify with different cultural clusters. The framework will help you to anticipate possible similarities and differences. Though again I caution you: the previous chapters have deepened our appreciation of the perils of over-generalising when it comes to geography as a singular cultural identifier.

There will be variances across different people in the same country and across different countries listed in the geographical clusters. We cannot presume that all Latin Europeans are passionately expressive, that all Germanic Europeans hate small talk and that all South Asians are comfortable with hierarchy. That would be what sociologists refer to as an ecological fallacy – the mistake of assuming that what is true for a group is true for the individual members of that group.

The table overleaf shows the 10 largest cultural groupings, or global clusters, in the world – based on the work of the CQ Center, which further expands on Simcha Simi Ronen and Oded Shenkar's eight clusters.

Anglo	Australia, Canada, New Zealand, UK, US, etc.
Arab	Bahrain, Egypt, Jordan, Kuwait, Lebanon, Morocco, Saudi Arabia, UAE, etc.
Confucian Asia	China, Hong Kong, Japan, Singapore, South Korea, Taiwan, etc.
Eastern Europe	Albania, Czech Republic, Greece, Hungary, Mongolia, Poland, Russia, etc.
Germanic Europe	Austria, Belgium, Germany, Netherlands, etc.
Latin America	Argentina, Bolivia, Brazil, Chile, Colombia, Costa Rica, Mexico, etc.
Latin Europe	France, French-speaking Canada, Italy, Portugal, Spain, etc.
Nordic Europe	Denmark, Finland, Iceland, Norway, Sweden, etc.
Sub-Saharan Africa	Ghana, Kenya, Namibia, Nigeria, Zambia, Zimbabwe, etc.
Southern Asia	India, Indonesia, Malaysia, Philippines, Thailand, etc.

© Cultural Intelligence Center, used by permission

IDENTITY: INDIVIDUALISM VERSUS COLLECTIVISM

Identity in the context of cultural values refers to how we see ourselves in relation to a group – be it family, friends, a business group or a larger community. Expression of identity can have a profound influence on how societies function.

Individualistic cultures emphasise the needs of the individual over the needs of the group as a whole. Independence is highly valued as individuals' rights tend to take a higher precedence. In such societies, people often place greater importance on being assertive, standing out and being unique.

This contrasts with collectivist cultures where people might sacrifice their own comfort for the greater good. Collectivism highlights the importance of the group through social cooperation. Characteristics such as being dependable, generous and helpful to others are of greater importance than individual needs.

Cross-cultural psychologists have observed that people from individualist cultures describe themselves differently compared to those from collectivist cultures. Psychosocial specialist Kendra Cherry says people from individualistic cultures are likely to present themselves in terms of their unique personal characteristics and traits – they might say, 'I am results-oriented, analytical and athletic'. She suggests that this can be contrasted with self-descriptions from people living in collectivist societies, who would be more likely to say something like, 'I am a good husband and loyal friend'.

I recall the story of Farid, a friend and neighbour, who was passionate about acting. He was expressive, confident and talented and had good prospects to pursue a career in the performing arts. Living in Dubai with his family of Pakistani heritage, he had researched and mentally shortlisted several prominent academies around the world to apply to after graduating from high school.

Farid's father was a hugely successful business owner with powerful investors and a growing international portfolio. It was expected that Farid, as the eldest and only son, would step into his father's business and be groomed to one day take the reins. When the conversation about higher education was tabled over a family dinner, acting as a profession was swiftly written off on his behalf.

The collectivist way of parenting is to consider everyone in the family structure, not just the one child. What the child studies, where they study and their ultimate career journey is decided as a collective. The key consideration is what is best for everyone. Farid's father's success was built on a strong motivation to provide well for his children and offer them the best life that he could.

Tasked with a weighty decision to choose between his own dream and that of his parents, Farid decided to sidestep his personal plans so he wouldn't disappoint his family. He eventually went to Chicago to study business and returned to start his career under his father's direction in the business.

In traditional collectivist societies, ties to the extended family group are strong. The choice of spouse can also be heavily influenced, if not decided, by parents or the greater community. With the emphasis on kinship, individuals are more likely to turn to family and friends for support during difficult times. Collectivist families are often characterised by the coexistence and interdependence of several generations within a household.

Collectivist cultures include Korea, Japan, Indonesia, India, Argentina and Brazil.

Nuclear families are a feature of individualistic societies which breed a nature of self-reliance, as children are encouraged to be independent early in life. Dependency is deemed less than ideal. Parents instil values and guide their children to make choices for themselves. Children's innate talents are supported, and they are encouraged to pursue their personal dreams.

Individualistic cultures include Australia, the United States, Germany and South Africa.

Motivating across the individualist–collectivist value dimension

People across the identity dimension are motivated differently. Individualists are driven by autonomy and personal accountability and wish to be recognised for individual achievements. Being singled out for recognition and reward is a strong motivator in individualist cultures, which in turn spurs a competitive mindset. A strong desire to attain personal goals drives an ambition of self-fulfilment.

Collectivists, on the other hand, are compelled by common goals and tend to emphasise relationships. They will consider the impact on the group and work to build consensus in a team. Being singled out for recognition and reward is demotivating in a culture where you are taught to blend in. Social harmony takes high priority as people take action on what is instinctively best for the group, be it in the context of a family, a team or community.

We all like to be recognised and receive validation for our efforts. How this is done needs careful consideration in light of cultural leanings in an organisation. For rewards programs to be effective in motivating the achievement of desired results, businesses need to understand the preferences of the people involved.

Individualist culture traits

- Emphasis on individual goals and rights.
- Often refer to 'I'.
- Claim the right to express personal views.
- Self-reliance is of great importance.
- Being dependent upon others is often considered embarrassing.
- Emphasis on standing out and being unique.

Collectivist culture traits

- Emphasis on community needs ahead of individual needs.
- Often refer to 'we'.
- Families and communities have a central role.
- Emphasis on personal relationships and belonging.
- Prioritise collective views.
- Strive for conformity and prefer to blend in.

Cultural clusters

INDIVIDUALISM Emphasis on individual goals and individual rights		**COLLECTIVISM** Emphasis on group goals and personal relationships
Anglo	Eastern Europe	Arab
Germanic Europe	Latin Europe	Confucian Asia
Nordic Europe		Latin America
		Southern Asia*
		Sub-Saharan Africa

* Significant variation within the cluster
© Cultural Intelligence Center, used by permission

Be curious

Your cultural lens

- Do you think of yourself primarily as an individual or primarily as a member of specific groups?

- Do you desire autonomy and personal accountability, or do you prefer to work towards group goals?

- 'I' or 'we' – what features in your thinking and expression? Does it change depending on the group you associate with at any given time?

Curious about others

- Can you identify the preference of others in your groups?

- Do they share your preference or are there differences? How do the differences show up?

- How might you bridge those differences?

AUTHORITY: LOW VERSUS HIGH POWER DISTANCE

The authority dimension refers to power structures and societal expectations and acceptance of the distance between leaders and followers. Authority is rooted in deeply held cultural values that permeate all segments of society, from family to business to government.

A low power distance culture is a more flat, egalitarian approach where power is dispersed. In low power distance societies, people tend not to accept situations where power is skewed or distributed unequally.

High power distance is conversely characterised by hierarchical structures. Such constructs tend to grant considerable power to those in positions of authority, be it the head of a family, those at the top of an organisation or leaders of a nation.

We can look to very recent history to illustrate this cultural dimension that speaks to deference to authority. As the world was spinning into crisis during the 2020 pandemic, cultural traits were evident in the highest levels of authority – namely government. World over, we witnessed different styles of engagement between national leaders and their citizens.

High power distance governments such as China, Korea and Singapore issued stricter behavioural guidelines for their people during periods of lockdown. Citizens were vigilantly monitored for social distancing and penalised for deviance from the rules. According to Sung-Yoon Lee, an international relations professor at the Fletcher School at Tufts University, traditions of Confucianism in these countries gave 'the paternalistic state a freer hand in exercising authority' during the pandemic. He suggested that most people living in these cultures willingly submit themselves to authority during an emergency and few complain.

Meanwhile, in Australia, federal and state officials were publicly questioned and openly criticised for their pandemic management policies. Autonomy is a much-cherished value in democratic societies and the declared crisis highlighted that power does not always persuade. Many responded adversely to the idea of active policing for disregard of social distancing regulations and felt they were capable of self-imposing.

Low power distance governments allow for more personal discretion through a sense of mutual obligation. Sweden's highly controversial approach to lockdown was driven by a framework of individual responsibility that rested on mutual trust. Swedish leaders encouraged self-regulation of social distancing rather than 'draconian' lockdown driven by a top-down control.

Australia is strongly representative of a low power distance society with an emphasis on equality. Other low power distance countries include the Scandinavian cluster and New Zealand. High power distance countries include the Arab countries, the Philippines, Singapore, Malaysia, China, Japan and Russia.

Keep in mind that power is at play in all relationships in society – parents and children, teachers and students, doctors and patients, managers and subordinates. Power is nuanced by the culturally accepted distribution. The smaller the power distance the more consultative and equal the approach. In higher power distance relationships, people will be expected to be guided or more explicitly told what to do by authority figures. Recognising power distance can tell a tale of the hierarchy within a group.

Decision-making across the high–low power distance value dimension

Having started at the highest level of power, let's look at the influence of power distance on business and more specifically decision-making, where variances across this cultural dimension are more pronounced. This dimension is measured between leaders in authoritative positions and followers who acquiesce to that power.

From my experience of designing leadership programs for client businesses, the topic of decision-making is raised frequently by stakeholders – both leaders and followers. 'He needs to be more solutions oriented.' 'She needs to take ownership.' These are just some of the common gripes I hear from business leaders. The general assumption is that these individuals are not capable of problem-solving. On the flip side, subordinates often counter the criticism suggesting that their leader is not delegating the author-ity or accepting solutions put forward by team members.

Top-down leadership is ever-present in high power distance societies, rooted in deeply held values in the larger culture. As a result, people demand those in power take responsibility. Leaders are expected to make decisions, resolve disputes and ultimately have the final say. This breeds a culture of compliance for subordinates who are less likely to challenge authority, be empowered to make firm commitments and take ownership of decision-making.

Subordinates shaped by a high power distance culture need clearer operating guidelines in which ownership is clearly allocated, authority frameworks are provided and expectations are outlined explicitly. Leaders shaped by the same cultural dynamic need to learn to delegate and adopt a more consultative management style with their team members.

Confusion occurs when different styles come to the table. I have worked in government organisations in the UAE with a prevalent collaborative working culture among senior executive teams in the office. Decisions were made collectively with strong reasoning. However, it was a frequent occurrence for government leaders, gathered at a late-night *majlis*, to override any well-thought-through recommendations or detailed justifications without explanation. A form of council, the *majlis* serves as a traditional forum for members of an exclusively senior, chiefly male community to raise important matters with elders and Sheikhs. The power distance with this group is more exaggerated and the difference in status and authority are typical of Arab culture.

Lower power distance cultures prefer a collaborative approach, recognising that everyone is entitled to voice their opinion and put forward their ideas. Open discussion and debate lead to collective problem-solving.

We become accustomed to underlying power structures in all tiers of society. Much goes without saying through unwritten rules of engagement. When people of different cultures come together, they will act according to their cultural orientation unless told otherwise. There is potential for misalignment across the power distances. The rules of engagement need to be clear to bring everyone on the same page. Tools such as guidelines on decision-making, authority matrices and training can go a long way towards avoiding confusion and a collision of power in business.

Low power distance culture traits

- Strive to equalise power distribution.
- Expect that everyone be listened to regardless of rank.
- Reject autocratic leadership.
- Minimal hierarchy.
- Inclination to forgo formality.
- All strata of society mix easily and with comfort.

High power distance culture traits

- Societal acceptance that power is distributed unequally.
- Defer to higher ranks with power granted to those in authority.
- Greater respect for authority and hierarchy.
- Hierarchy prevails through class and ranking systems.
- Tendency towards formality.
- Differences in status are recognised and respected.

Cultural clusters

LOW POWER DISTANCE		HIGH POWER DISTANCE
Emphasis on equality; shared decision-making		Emphasis on differences in status; superiors make decisions
Anglo	Confucian Asia	Arab
Germanic Europe	Eastern Europe*	Latin America
Nordic Europe	Latin Europe	Southern Asia*
	Sub-Saharan Africa	

* Significant variation within the cluster
© Cultural Intelligence Center, used by permission

Be curious

Your cultural lens

- Do you prefer a flat, egalitarian approach to leadership or a more top-down, hierarchical leadership style?

- Do you prefer formality, or do you opt to forgo formality in favour of less formal settings?

- Are you comfortable sharing viewpoints with seniors and/or hearing viewpoints from subordinates?

Curious about others

- Does your preference change when you report to others versus when you lead? If so, how?

- What is the prevalent culture in your company? Is reaching a consensus, where everyone has a voice, of importance or are some afraid to openly challenge authority?

- Can you identify those around you who score differently on this value dimension? How?

EXPRESSION: NEUTRAL VERSUS AFFECTIVE

The value dimension of expression reveals preferences for neutral versus affective expression. As humans, we are emotional beings. Emotion is expressed differently across cultures. Whether or not we express emotions overtly, we all have them.

Neutral cultures suppress explicit displays of emotion through controlled expression. Social norms dictate that feelings should remain hidden behind an impartial facade. In contrast, affective cultures emphasise expressive communication and members openly share their feelings.

As I enter a luxury watch boutique in Melbourne, Antonello greets me with a welcoming smile, sparkly eyes and arms outstretched as if he's about to hug me. We don't know each other yet. In fact, I am there on a mystery shopping exercise. Instead of hugging he extends his hand, offers his name and suggests that he take me on a small tour of his boutique. His passion for the brand is contagious. His expression is theatrical but genuine. His tone is excited, and his gestures are animated and confident. After 20 minutes of enthusiastic storytelling, I'm romanced and almost ready to drop several thousands of dollars on a watch I know I can't afford and don't really want or need.

Antonello is of Italian origin. His expressive communication style and outward demonstration of passion is characteristic of the Latin European cultural orientation towards affective expression.

Just across the border from Italy, in neighbouring Germany, it's the norm to disguise what you are feeling or thinking. Being cool and controlled is admired. Across the Baltic Sea, Swedes share the same sensibilities and several thousand miles east, the Japanese orientation towards neutral expression is even stronger. Imagine if, in my place at the watch boutique, there was a potential customer who preferred less expressive communications. People of neutral cultures such as Germany, Sweden and Japan may feel overwhelmed by Antonello's exuberance. As they habitually refrain from open displays of emotion, they are unlikely to show offence.

Cultures that are affective in expression include Italy, Spain and Latin-American countries.

When I am received by a retail sales professional of Asian culture, it's unlikely that I will be greeted with a great deal of enthusiasm; even though they may feel excited to have a potential customer in their store, their outward expression is reserved. In fact, Antonello's Mandarin-speaking colleagues find it immensely difficult to hold eye contact and offer their name. This is where expression overlaps with authority. An accepted and expected distance in power – in this case, between the customer and the service professional – prevents some cultures from asserting themselves. Restraint is in fact a sign of respect.

Cultures that are neutral in expression include Japan, the UK, Sweden, the Netherlands and Finland.

Cultivating relationships across the neutral–affective value dimension

Emotional intelligence (EQ), a term popularised by psychologist Daniel Goleman, is an essential capability in establishing effective relationships; it is a pivotal factor for personal and professional success.

In Australia, outward demonstration of enthusiasm is the norm in the workplace. Expression of feelings is accepted – in fact, encouraged – making it relatively easy to read someone's emotions.

However, as we have now established through this cultural value dimension, EQ is culture bound. In culturally complex situations, establishing relationships is dependent on understanding the cultural value differences involved. Determining whether a culture is neutral or affective helps with planning for cross-cultural engagement.

As I witnessed with one of my clients – an Australian business acquired by a Japanese company and reporting to Japanese board members – the potential for frustration with variances across this dimension can be high. Japan is representative of Confucian Asian culture where people rarely express emotions at work. The Japanese do not gesture very much while speaking; their body language is largely restrained. Their communication pattern is very indirect and far less verbose than that of Anglo cultures. Smiling can indicate happiness but also an attempt to cover awkwardness to diffuse an uncomfortable situation in favour of maintaining harmony.

The Australian management team collectively leans towards affective expression; meetings with their Japanese counterparts can be full of indecipherable moments. Lack of response or enthusiasm from the head of the table can be confusing as well as disheartening. If the Australian team communicates in their naturally expressive style with animated gestures and louder, fast-paced communication, it's likely to be overwhelming for the receiver.

Gauging when to be more restrained and considered and when to be more outgoing and social in intercultural interactions is key to cultivating meaningful relationships. Establishing common ground by matching someone's speech patterns – such as tone, tempo and volume – is a great way to keep a comfortable rhythm in communication. If someone is slow and deliberate, matching their pace and tone will maintain a sense of synchronicity. You might even go as far as to match someone's breathing to keep a relaxed atmosphere. Pausing for a moment of mindfulness attention to observe the person in front of you will help you to slow down and connect more purposefully. These learned techniques can become second nature and go a long way to establish a comfortable and respectful rapport.

Neutral culture traits

- Restrained expression of emotion.
- Show of emotions considered inappropriate.
- Steady tone of voice; formal communication.
- Restrained physical gestures.
- Self-control is valued.
- May appear cool, aloof, intellectually driven.

Affective culture traits

■ Outward expression of emotion.

■ Enthusiastic and spontaneous.

■ Exaggerated tone; informal communication.

■ Wider range of physical gestures and facial expressions.

■ Debate is valued.

■ May appear emotional and driven by feelings.

Cultural clusters

NEUTRAL/NON-EXPRESSIVE		AFFECTIVE/EXPRESSIVE
Emphasis on non-emotional communication; hiding feelings		Emphasis on expressive communication; sharing feelings
Confucian Asia	Anglo*	Arab
Eastern Europe	Southern Asia	Latin America
Germanic Europe		Latin Europe
Nordic Europe		Sub-Saharan Africa

* Significant variation within the cluster
© Cultural Intelligence Center, used by permission

Be curious

Your cultural lens

- Do you tend to hide your emotions or show them? Do people find it easy to read your emotions?

- Do you outwardly display enthusiasm and passion in the workplace, or are you more reserved and cautious about expressing what you really feel?

- Do you love a good debate or are you more reflective?

- Do you know how to switch modes?

Curious about others

- Do you interact with cultures with a different orientation on the neutral–affective scale?

- Do you need to adjust your style when communicating with someone of a different preference? If so, how could you do this?

- What adjustments might you appreciate from others with a different cultural orientation?

COMMUNICATION: HIGH CONTEXT VERSUS LOW CONTEXT

This dimension highlights how cultures communicate on a spectrum of low context to high context. Low context cultures prefer explicit communication with an emphasis on the words spoken. High context cultures focus on the context around the words spoken, not just the literal meaning of them. Large variances across this spectrum have the potential to cause a high level of frustration in multicultural situations.

Low context communicators like to get to the point. They prefer clarity and orderly communication and will focus on the content of a message, both when delivering and receiving it. High context communicators, on the other hand, tend to speak around a point, leaving much to interpretation. As listeners, they are more likely to tune into the circumstances around which communication takes place, paying attention to tone, gestures and pauses.

The contrast of high and low context serves as a guide to understand patterns in communication. This can help us decode cross-cultural intent. It does not, however, suggest that all members of a culture communicate in the same way.

At an individual level, we may find that we lean strongly towards one style – though it is not always a case of one versus the other. In fact, our communication typically contains both modes. Our style can be situational, meaning that settings and relationships with those we communicate with will further guide our approach to conversation.

There is a quiet understanding in established groups that rely on a common background and understanding. These may be professional, social or religious. We can even look to a family that has grown and lived together. Members of such cultural groups already know what is expected and what to do and they do not need to exchange many words to understand one another. Such environments appear to be high context to a newcomer and can be difficult to break into. When I step into different client businesses across a range of industries, each one appears high context to me; initially I am not familiar with their social codes and inferences. I can't quite read between the lines.

At one point in my career I managed a large team across three different departments: marketing, sales and customer service. I can recount 10 different cultures in my team, including many Arab expatriate, Indian, Iranian, American and Irish members – and I am only counting national cultures at this point.

The senior leadership team that I reported to comprised an Australian chief executive, a British chief of finance and an Emirati chairperson. Our client base was equally diverse. Such was the cultural melting pot, Dubai, at the time, comprising a diverse and predominantly expatriate population. The team dynamics and daily interactions were laden with complexities in messaging that I frequently had to decipher, translate and untangle.

We had all communication styles in the mix. Layered with this we had differences across the cultural value dimensions. In part III of *Curious about Culture* we unpack the values – identity, authority, expression, communication, rules and achievement – independently. In real life, they don't show up autonomous of one another. In fact, these cultural values are related: they intersect, and they spin a complex web. Each team member's value orientations steered their communication preferences. Those hailing from particularistic cultures believed they could bend the rules as processes didn't apply to them. Accordingly, their reporting was jumbled and their delivery of project status updates in our team meetings was constrained by their inclination to talk around a point thereby often missing precise detail.

Those with a preference for equality rather than hierarchical structures combined with a low context communication style were not afraid to call out such shortcomings in the presence of a group. This left their counterparts feeling slighted from messaging that they interpreted to be confrontational and disrespectful. Cultures that typically value harmony will avoid direct conflict and confrontation as the relationship is the driving value. Such cultures may take offence to communication that appears blunt and rude. They value relationships with their peers, who they expect to have their back over loyalty to company reporting practices.

Is this painting a picture – one that perhaps you can start to relate to from your own cross-cultural interactions?

Within any group there are variances that call for an understanding of deeper subtleties and attention to underlying meaning and tone in communication. Knowing that Australians and New Zealanders belong to the Anglo cluster and are geographically so close, we might throw them into the same regional bucket for simplification as they share many commonalities. However, both nations have differing historical and environmental influences that result in some cultural differences, as my New Zealand clients never fail to remind me.

Compared to Australians, New Zealanders are relatively indirect communicators in that they are more considered and reserved in speech – some may even say tight-lipped. They are typically polite and try their best not to create conflict. Their orientation towards caution sways communicators to choose comparatively vague messaging to avoid seeming overly confrontational. Nevertheless, their style of communication is not so indirect that it has to be deciphered, especially when we compare them with cultures that are much further along the scale towards high context, such as Japan, China and Mexico.

Comparatively, New Zealanders may consider their Australian neighbours to be bold, direct and more confident in their speech. Any desire to sidestep confrontation would not hold them back from saying what they mean.

Communicating with meaning across the low to high context dimension

Our patterns and preferences in communication tend to be subconscious until we draw our attention to them. We have a default style, one that is familiar and comfortable, that we defer to when communicating with others. Communication is a process that conveys meaning. Meaningful communication is a two-way process: it involves both the entity delivering and the entity receiving that message. It cannot, therefore, be entirely speaker centric. To be truly effective we need to divert our focus to the receiver's understanding of the message.

I love the acronym coined by James Wagstaffe at TED: ABC, or 'audience before content'. I would go as far as to say 'audience before *communicator*'. Make it audience-centric to be truly effective.

As a first step you can become aware of your orientation on the communication dimension. To then be relevant and meaningful across culture, look to the orientation of those you intend to address. Look to your communication intent. What is the goal of this communication? What do you hope to achieve? Accordingly, shift out of your default mode to extend yourself to the orientation of others.

Low context culture traits

- Explicit and linear communication.
- Words are valued above their context.
- Tend to favour written communications.
- Disagreements are less personal and conflict is dealt with rationally.

High context culture traits

- Communication tends to be indirect and harmonious.
- Large amount of information is provided in a non-verbal manner, e.g. gestures, pauses, facial expressions.

- Tend to favour oral communications; 'unwritten' rules can be assumed.
- Prefer to avoid direct confrontation.

Cultural clusters

LOW CONTEXT/DIRECT		HIGH CONTEXT/INDIRECT
Emphasis on explicit communication (words)		Emphasis on indirect communication (tone, context)
Anglo	Eastern Europe	Arab
Germanic Europe	Latin America	Confucian Asia
Nordic Europe	Latin Europe	Southern Asia*
		Sub-Saharan Africa

* Significant variation within the cluster
© Cultural Intelligence Center, used by permission

Be curious

Your cultural lens

- Do you prefer communication that is explicit, direct and clear or is your communication style more indirect, emphasising harmony and saving face?

- Do you seek clarity through words? Do you rely upon the written word more often than not?

- Do you recognise implied messages from others – what is being said verbally and what is being communicated through non-verbal cues?

Curious about others

- How might your orientation be similar or different to those in your social ecosystem, your friends and work associates?

- Do differences go unrecognised or create confusion or conflict?

- How might you facilitate a dialogue with different cultural groups to agree upon a communication style?

RULES: UNIVERSALISM VERSUS PARTICULARISM

The rules dimension highlights the extent to which people prefer to apply the same standards to everyone versus making exceptions for friends and family across the scale of universalism and particularism. Universalism is based on an underlying belief that universally agreed rules apply to everyone in society. This approach places high importance on adherence to standards, laws and policies. Particularism, on the other hand, allows for exceptions to rules in special circumstances with a greater emphasis on relationship obligations.

My friend, Herman, is a property manager responsible for a portfolio of residential buildings. Amid the financial stresses of the 2020 global pandemic he was inundated with pleas from a large number of tenants and their real estate agents. Some tenants wanted to downsize: three-bedroom units to two, two-bedrooms to one, and so on. Some tenants needed to defer payment of their monthly rent. Others had been watching market trends and attempted to renegotiate rental agreements.

Despite the administrative hurdles he was inviting for himself, Herman was determined to address each case individually over the simpler option of applying the state's published regulations as a blanket rule. He prioritised his relationships with his tenants. His phone was ringing incessantly as he juggled calls from numerous tenants. He told me, 'Each person's situation is different; some are genuinely facing financial difficulty. I can't treat them the same, I need to help them all'. He was reluctant to change his approach.

Raised in a Latino culture, Herman migrated to Australia from Chile with his family when he was very young. His particularistic attitude suggests that he inherited his family's value perspectives, despite the social influences of from where he was raised. South American cultures are highly relationship-oriented, and people are thereby more open to approach matters with a 'case by case' view, based on prevailing circumstances.

In contrast, Australia's highly universalist approach, representative of Anglo culture, prescribes that the same standards apply to everyone. Someone with a universalist orientation would have tackled the situation differently, with a broad-brush approach to applying stipulated regulations across the board.

In particularistic societies, it is extremely important to build good relationships with people to get things done. The adage 'it's not what you know but who you know' is exemplified in the practice of *wasta*. An Arabic term loosely translated as 'clout', *wasta* is a valuable currency that can open doors. Whether you are trying to get a foot in the door for an interview or bidding to get the attention of someone of influence in government or business, the power of a personal introduction – *wasta* – is that connection that can help you succeed.

Typical particularistic cultures include Latin America, Africa, the Middle East, Russia and China.

Rules apply to everyone and everyone is treated the same in universalist societies. As meritocracies, it is primarily your personal credentials that will get you into the university or school of your choice, or land you a job. Relationships are important, though rules have greater priority as people aim to be fair in all respects.

Typical universalist cultures include Australia, the US, Canada, the UK, the Netherlands, Germany, Switzerland and Scandinavia.

Negotiating across the universalism–particularism value dimension

There is potential for a strong clash of cultures when negotiating with people of different cultural convictions. 'Negotiation' sounds like a heavy term but, in fact, we encounter situations that require some form of negotiation on a daily basis, both in our personal and professional lives: from discussing the terms of a property contract, to brokering terms of engagement with a client, to agreeing on travel plans with a group of friends.

Imagine yourself in the Grand Bazaar in Turkey, haggling with a friendly trader over a must-have rug that you can already picture in your lounge. According to Turkish tradition, the price is inflated, and the expectation is that you will bargain for a better price. Ultimately the price settles where the buyer and seller agree. While haggling might be an enjoyable pursuit when in a new environment, people with a universalist preference would struggle with this as an everyday encounter. In universalist societies there is little or no room to negotiate on price as there is an understanding that rates are typically standard and fair.

If two people are negotiating together or simply working together on a project and their underlying orientations and expectations differ, there is potential for a great deal of frustration. Understanding the underlying value system across cultures goes a long way towards effective problem-solving and negotiation across cultures.

If you are negotiating in a particularistic culture, you will need to be flexible with agreements to avoid frustration when things don't quite go to your plan. Investing time in building good relationships is key to building a common understanding and eventually getting things done.

If you are negotiating in a universalist culture, you will need to make sure that there are clear agreements and processes in place. The focus is on objective decision-making and clear explanations.

Universalist culture traits

- The same standards apply to everyone.
- Emphasis on rules.
- Expectation to be treated like everyone else.
- Fixed pricing with little or no room to manoeuvre.

Particularistic culture traits

- Rules are malleable in special circumstances.
- Emphasis on relationships.
- Expectation to be treated differently.
- Bartering is commonplace.

Cultural clusters

UNIVERSALISM
Emphasis on rules;
standards that apply to everyone

PARTICULARISM
Emphasis on specifics;
unique standards based on relationships

Anglo	Eastern Europe	Arab
Germanic Europe	Latin Europe	Confucian Asia*
Nordic Europe		Latin America
		Southern Asia
		Sub-Saharan Africa

* Significant variation within the cluster
© Cultural Intelligence Center, used by permission

Be curious

Your cultural lens

- Do you believe that rules apply equally to everyone?

- Do you prioritise rules over relationships or vice versa? Do you believe that rules can be modified to account for individual circumstances, at least for family and friends?

- In your experience, is it *who* you know or *what* you know that prevails?

Curious about others

- Can you identify someone in your network with a different preference to your own?

- How does this difference present itself in cross-cultural exchanges? How might you bridge the gap?

- Are there any opportunities that this difference presents?

15

ACHIEVEMENT: COOPERATIVE VERSUS COMPETITIVE

The achievement dimension alludes to a cultural orientation on the cooperative to competitive scale. It is a means to an end as this dimension sheds light on prioritisation of tasks versus relationships in achieving results. This is not to say that one orientation is more or less achievement focused or in fact more or less successful than another.

Cultures that are competitive have a task-first focus and tend to be more assertive and results driven. The modern-day world is highly competitive. We are constantly competing against one another in some form. We are encouraged to outperform our peers from the school playing field to the exam room and the sports arena to the job market. Most of Western business is largely organised around a competitive orientation. We often hear that it's about survival of the fittest. The US is one of the most competitive cultures in the world, followed by other Anglo and Germanic cultures. Competition is a driving force that values ambition, action and results.

Cultures that are cooperative in nature place high priority on collaboration through establishing and nurturing relationships. Cooperative societies are driven by guiding principles that prioritise collaboration and value human force. Nordic countries such as Denmark and Sweden are among the highest on the cooperative scale. Results are of equal importance in cooperative and competitive cultures; however, in cooperative cultures the emphasis is on collective achievement recognising that outcomes are the result of cooperative alliances and groups of people working together.

Those who sit on each end of the spectrum are not necessarily in opposition: they may be working towards the same goals, but merely approaching them differently. This can create a sense of misalignment or incompatibility in a business setting that may not be true.

Arab and Confucian-Asian cultures are moderately positioned on the scale. Some years back I was invited to participate in the inauguration of a dedicated new pearl market in the Chinese city of Zhuji. Representing a Dubai government entity, I was there to honour their invitation and strengthen liaisons between the two trading hubs. After a ceremony of ribbon cutting and speeches, I accompanied senior officials to our scheduled lunch meeting.

My colleague and I were led to a private dining room with 10 Chinese officials where lunch played out over a ritualised five course meal. The entire occasion must have lasted nearly two and a half hours. Since most around the table couldn't speak English and my Mandarin is limited to a basic vocabulary of *ni-hao* and *xie xie*, our exchanges were restricted to occasional smiles, nods of the head and very little direct conversation.

As someone who is treading a fine line between two ends of the relationship-task spectrum, this called for some patience on my part. I am a big believer that people work for people, and that nurturing relationships is central to any business liaison. That said, I am also hugely action oriented. I would have happily combined lunch with a business conversation.

The ceremony of dining together was an obligatory step in strengthening ties between the two governmental organisations. The dominant cultural belief of Confucianism emphasises interdependence of relationships, relying heavily upon trust and mutual obligation. This manifests in Chinese society as a concept called *guanxi* meaning 'connections'. The key to success is through established connections, be they personal, familial, political or social relationships. Appreciating that the Chinese, in general, are comparatively longer-term planners, their desire for progress was based on a different timeline than my own preference to return to my organisation with confirmation of immediate progress.

Establishing trust across the cooperative–competitive value dimension

Cultures that are cooperatively inclined will form trust on the basis of a relationship. Relationships take time to establish. Cultures that lean more strongly towards a competitive orientation will establish trust on the basis of results, focusing attention on immediate triumphs.

This orientation is easy to detect in business settings. When you next meet a business acquaintance, a client or a supplier, observe if it's a 'down to business' approach or if time is invested up-front in checking in on personal matters. This is not to say that people who are competitively inclined don't value relationships; it is just more likely that they will jump to the matter at hand and save the personal banter for later or over a social occasion.

We may be more comfortable at one end of the spectrum than the other and identify strongly with one side of the scale. However, some flexibility is called for to establish trust across cultural orientations. Demonstrating adaptability in response to the differing needs and values of the people with whom we interact will go a long way to cultivating trust.

There are common denominators of trust that translate across all cultures, such as integrity, respect and honesty. In the case of my China visit, we could be quick to label the social courtesies as bureaucratic. They were however hugely important in establishing relations. As members of a cooperative culture the Chinese officials both expected and appreciated my participation in their ceremonious lunch – it was a sign of respect.

The key to success lies in being cognisant of when personal banter can go a long way in establishing a relationship versus getting straight to the task at hand or vice versa. If a meeting is scheduled to be held in a café or over lunch, this is a signal that suggests a relaxed atmosphere with room for social conversation compared to a formal business setting.

Learning about the cultures you work with will offer insights into motivations within a team or across counterparts. Be mindful that an individual may be acting upon the cultural dominance of the organisation they represent.

Australia's informal 'matey' culture indicates a social leaning towards collaboration, however the business ecosphere is somewhat Americanised with a competitive tendency. There is little protocol in business settings, conversation flows easily and there is a task-first slant.

Also belonging to the Anglo cluster, the British are comparatively more strongly driven by tradition and task orientation, seeming formal upfront but softening into an easygoing, friendly rhythm in subsequent encounters. They won't hesitate to direct a discussion when excessive non-business banter is slowing it down, and can do so with tactful humour.

Being attentive to this cultural dimension, you can take the lead from your counterpart and expand into their preference accordingly. In situations where you need to take the lead, a simple agreement on how you might spend scheduled time together can set the tone. This will pave your way to establishing rapport with ease.

Cooperative culture traits

- Prioritise relationships.
- Focus on human interaction.
- Relationship driven.
- Value collaboration.
- Seek acknowledgement of the group's collective efforts.

Competitive culture traits

- Prioritise tasks.
- Reward high performance.
- Results driven.
- Value assertiveness.
- Seek individual praise and recognition.

Cultural clusters

COOPERATIVE

Emphasis on collaboration,
nurturing and family

COMPETITIVE

Emphasis on competition,
assertiveness and achievement

Nordic Europe	Arab	Anglo
Sub-Saharan Africa	Confucian Asia	Germanic Europe
	Eastern Europe	
	Latin America	
	Latin Europe	
	Southern Asia*	

* Significant variation within the cluster
© Cultural Intelligence Center, used by permission

Be curious

My cultural lens

- Do you prioritise relationships or tasks?

- Do you like to work independently, or do you prefer to work collaboratively?

- Do you seek individual recognition, or would you feel fulfilled through acknowledgement as a contributor to group efforts?

Curious about others

- What is the culture of your organisation and your specific department?

- Are you aligned to the prevalent culture or is there a variance?

- Can you detect the preference of your co-workers? Are they aligned to the prevalent culture? Is there a way to bridge the gap?

PART IV
LOOKING BEYOND

Now that you have come to the end of this journey of cultural exploration with me, I hope that *Curious about Culture* has gone some way to quenching your thirst for knowledge.

Just as the view through the kaleidoscopic lens is unique to each viewer, our view of culture is unique to each of us. With the concepts offered in this book you will have acquired awareness of your own filters on culture. You have had the opportunity to refocus your lens on culture. You now also have broader vocabulary to describe your cultural values.

I prefaced this book with the suggestion that to connect across cultures with people of diverse backgrounds we first need to understand our own cultural identities and how they mould our lens of the world. I trust that the perspectives I have offered through a combination of anecdotes and suggestions have helped you achieve this.

It is now time to connect the dots from the stories within these pages to your own intercultural experiences to draw some patterns.

Have you dedicated time to pause and reflect at the series of introspective questions listed in the 'Be curious' sections that conclude each chapter? If not, I urge you to do so now. You can revisit these sections over time in the context of different environments and the diverse groups to which you belong across your personal and professional spheres.

I will now take you a step further on this journey so that you can apply your refined lens in order to boost your cross-cultural effectiveness.

16

FRAMING YOUR CURIOSITY

Throughout the previous chapters and true to the title of this book, I have encouraged you to be curious. Curiosity is key to meaningfully deepening our cross-cultural connectivity. We can demonstrate curiosity by asking deliberate questions to gain useful perceptions, free of judgement. Look to frame your curiosity with respectful, open questions, rather than questions that project an assumption.

'Do you speak Mandarin?' This is a close-ended question that can only be answered with one word – 'yes' or 'no'. The question is charged with an assumption, often based on racial profile. You can reframe this as an open-ended question avoiding conjecture – 'Do you speak any other languages?' or 'Which other languages do you speak?'

By now we have established that we all have many facets to our cultural identities. Let us not reduce people to a singular facet of their cultural identity.

For example, asking someone 'Are you Muslim?', because they have an Arabic sounding name is frankly rude. Information about someone's country of origin or their name does not give you permission to conclude what they believe in. Faith is a very personal filter for some.

Think about why you are pursuing such lines of enquiry in the first place. For those being asked, these questions feel loaded. We need to ask ourselves what motivates our desire to know about someone's identity, faith or ethnicity. If it is to confirm a hunch, steer away and save everyone an awkward moment. Did you pick up on an accent, or a racial profile that piqued your interest? Think of a situation when you were recognised by a feature ascribed to you. Go back to that moment and remember what it felt like being asked a question laden with assumption or limiting notions. What would you have liked others to know about you instead?

If you have time for a deep and meaningful conversation, considered and carefully framed questions will lead to a more comfortable and open dialogue that can go beyond the surface. If it is just a passing encounter, hold back the small talk and enjoy the richness of the moment.

I will admit, there are times when I can't hold back my curiosity – especially if I have an urge to build a connection or show that we have something in common. However, if we assume a similarity or even a difference, we run the risk of causing offence. You can frame your questions around a detectable trait and take it away from the person. Examples could include: 'Did I pick up an accent?' 'What is the origin of your name?' 'What is your family heritage?'

In a social setting, with the advantage of time, you can wait for the topic to surface organically. Through general social conversation, people tend to volunteer stories about childhood, travel and study. We know that culture is omnipresent and entwining in our cultural narratives. In chapter 9, 'The national dimension', I referred to food and sport as examples of shared interests. These make great conversation topics along with music interests, movies, art and so on. Keeping it simple and light encourages a natural rhythm of dialogue.

You will recall that I shared my daughter's very personal story to illustrate that asking 'Where are you from?' is not a great icebreaker. Asking 'Where are you *really* from?' is not just downright awkward, but will prevent you from making friends of cultural strangers. Underpinning your curiosity with active listening will help you determine if there's an opportunity to expand the conversation. If your inquisitiveness is received with positivity, that is your cue to go deeper. If your curiosity is not received with the openness and enthusiasm you had hoped for, read the signals and accept the answer you are given and don't probe any further.

I will conclude this chapter with a list of indicators that suggest when it can be a good time to actively demonstrate your curiosity and when not. You may be able to add more from your own experiences.

Be curious

When to be openly curious

- If it is someone in your immediate work or social circle.
- If you are in a one-on-one setting or a small group.
- When someone is noticeably conversational.
- When someone volunteers information about their personal culture.
- When your inquisitiveness is received with positivity.
- When you share a common language of understanding.

When it is best to refrain from open curiosity

- If it is a brief or passing encounter.
- When there is a large group of listeners.
- When someone is clearly not engaging in conversation.
- When your enquiry is not met with enthusiasm.
- When someone's body language is noticeably closed off.
- If you do not share the same level of understanding through a common language.

17

REFOCUSING CULTURAL FILTERS IN THE WORKPLACE

In part II of *Curious about Culture*, we unpacked the filters of gender, generation, faith, education, language and the national dimension to understand the multiple layers that construct our cultural identities.

As a first step, reflecting on each of these concepts helps to shed light on your own cultural identity. Secondly, it serves to better understand people around you. Carefully framed, each of these concepts makes for a discussion point with your various social groups. I will take this a step further into the professional sphere to provide you with some suggestions on how to identify these themes within the structure of your organisation. I will also offer some recommended approaches on how to address cultural disparities. It may appear that the ideas I propose are outside of your sphere of immediate influence or that the responsibility sits 'above your paygrade'. However, in truth, you don't have to be in a leadership position to demonstrate personal leadership. You can initiate change by sharing your knowledge in a solutions-oriented manner and communicating a rational need for it.

Applying the exercise from part I, 'Your circle of trust', to different teams in your organisation is a great place to start. From leadership teams to departmental teams, from the board of directors to project teams, you can reflect on the diversity within those groups. Furthermore, you can start to understand how this impacts the organisational culture at large. A company culture can be swayed by the collective and predominant thinking of those who have strong influence in the organisation. When you pick up the metaphoric kaleidoscopic lens you will start to see patterns.

You may access the template entitled 'The Circle of Trust for Teams' from the online toolkit (please see details on page 141). Once you have completed this, consider what it tells you at a first glance. Then take a closer look at each of the six filters and consider how these might show up in your organisation.

Gender

Look around the table at your next team meeting, be it departmental or a cross-functional project team. Consider if there is under-representation of one gender and over-representation of another. Note who is invited to the table. Who is chairing the meeting? Who is invited to participate in key strategic matters? Look to the distribution of responsibilities across genders. Identify the gender hierarchy in your organisation; is it balanced or is it skewed? Do the answers to these questions uncover a story?

Benchmark the current status quo vis-a-vis where you want your organisation to be. This desired change should to be planned deliberately, just like other strategic initiatives in your business.

No matter how positive the intentions, all good ideas fall by the wayside without a trackable, measurable plan. Articulate the goal, assign clear process ownership and accountability, determine a set of measurable initiatives and select a dedicated team.

Generation

Refer to the generational bands listed in chapter 5, 'The generational outlook' to profile your organisation or team. Identify which generations are represented more strongly. What are the traits of these generations that differentiate them from others?

Revisit the potential areas of conflict in the multi-generational workplace identified in the same chapter and start adding to that list. You can go further by facilitating a dialogue between a cross-section of generations and age categories in your organisation and ask them to contribute to this list.

Are you subconsciously catering only to the predominant generation at the expense of others? Consider also how different generational traits benefit the business. Combining differences in perspectives will be advantageous to the overall business.

Faith

Does your company nurture a culture of openness? How much do you know about your staff and peers? An employment contract is not a brief encounter – it symbolises a deeper engagement over a period of time. Therefore, this is one occasion that warrants finer knowledge of the people who work with and for you.

Once you are aware of the diversity in your organisation, you can work to expand the company holiday calendar. Acknowledge holidays that represent the religious beliefs held across the organisation. When you allow flexibility with leave and working hours, team members can fulfil obligations such as prayer and celebration of religious festivals without having to renounce these central aspects of their cultural identities. By creating space for faith, you will cultivate dedication and loyalty instead of forcing secrecy and isolation.

Education

What does your organisation value when looking to recruit talent? Is the emphasis on higher education and paper degrees, or experience, talent and attitude? Identify if you are geared to recruit a specific education biography or if you are truly welcoming of talent. Consider how you might align your recruitment channels, processes and criteria according to your findings.

When evaluating training needs in your organisation be sure that your analysis takes into consideration the different learning styles of people in your organisation. These may not be apparent to you, but you can deepen your understanding by simply engaging in a dialogue with people. Do your internal and external training consultants possess cultural sensitivity to be able to adapt to, and engage with, the cultural nuances in your team?

Language

How many languages are spoken in your organisation and does diversity enrich the social fabric of your business? What are the effects of the different language structures in the mix and how can cross-cultural understanding be improved?

In chapter 8, 'The language code', I gave an example of how the word 'please' is replaced with a polite and questioning intonation in languages where the word does not exist. The power lies in promoting understanding around how people express themselves and interact with others through day-to-day dialogue.

If you observe apparent diversity in a new group, you can make a point to start by asking how many, and which, languages are spoken in the group. This makes for interesting dialogue, especially if it provokes stories of living abroad and intercultural marriage that may have motivated someone to learn a language. More significantly, asking this question enables an understanding in the group that not everyone's first language is English, therefore allowing space for participants to reflect and process information and concepts.

The national dimension

Create opportunities for conversation among teams. It often surprises me how little colleagues know about one another when they come together in training programs or at social events. Create forums such as town hall meetings, breakfast meetings, happy hours and social activities to facilitate deeper dialogue so team members can really get to know and appreciate one another across the organisation. Use thoughtful conversation starters to bring to the surface some of the hidden layers of culture that lie beneath the visible line of the cultural iceberg.

All the while be mindful that nationality can trigger different associations for different people. Don't limit people to one national identity. Remember, many of us are living more than one culture at the same time – as I illustrated in chapter 9, 'The national dimension' with stories about hybrid identities, immigrants and third-culture kids.

***

Looking to the suggestions in this chapter, which of these cultural filters might you need to address in your organisation? Consider who you need to involve in the planning. You may have identified several areas of focus; you can prioritise in order of importance, readiness of your organisation and ease of implementation.

18

IDENTIFYING CULTURAL VALUES IN THE WORKPLACE

In part III of *Curious about Culture*, we explored six cultural values – identity, authority, expression, communication, rules and achievement. Our preference on these value dimensions influence how we interact with others, how we communicate and how we approach tasks.

How can you apply this understanding in your workplace with your peers and teams? You can simply transpose the cultural value dimensions from a personal focus to an organisational one.

Each cultural value dimension chapter concludes with a scale mapping the orientations along a continuum. Foster cross-cultural understanding by referring to this to open a discussion and identify both similarities and differences within your teams.

Know that one cultural value orientation is not better than another – it is merely different. The goal is not to change people's intrinsic preferences – as that is very unlikely to happen – but to bring awareness to everyone's default orientations, including your own. The next step is to enable people to bridge gaps with others who score differently on the scale. This awareness will enhance mutual understanding, nurture personal effectiveness and enable a culturally aware and cohesive team dynamic.

While supporting team members to uncover their personal cultural values, it is important to allow for diversity in the ecosystem of your business rather than expecting everyone to conform.

You can go on to facilitate a dialogue about the prevalent orientation across your organisation against these dimensions. What are the expectations that may arise as a result of these underlying dynamics? Is there an agreed social conduct and is this conduct made clear? Are different styles playing out in different parts of the organisation whereby teams take their cues from their line manager?

Is there a phenomenon of groupthink that calls to be recognised? This can occur when group members acquiesce to the collective thinking for the sake of conformity. It comes at a cost of independent and critical thinking.

The sets of 'Be curious' questions served to shed light on your personal preferences along the cultural values dimension. I encourage you to answer these questions if you haven't done so yet, as this will prepare you to reframe them from a personal to an organisational perspective. Here are some examples of how to reframe the questions and determine if your organisational culture is aligned with your people and vice versa.

Identity

Does the organisation encourage and reward individual achievement, or the collective group's outcomes?

Authority

What is the underlying power structure? Is it a top-down driven management hierarchy or are open discussion and debate encouraged from all tiers within the business?

Are channels for ideas sharing formal or informal, are they written or verbal and do they cut across hierarchies?

Expression

Is outward expression encouraged? Does everyone partake in open debate and constructive feedback, or do some hang back? How much time and opportunity is each person given to contribute to the discussion? Are people given the opportunity to contribute in different ways instead of speaking publicly?

Communication

Is the general communication style explicit, direct and clear? Which form of communication is preferred – written or oral?

Is confrontation expected and accepted or do people tend to beat around the bush? Is there agreement and clarity on what is considered respectful communication in a team?

Rules

Do the same standards apply to everyone across the organisation or are rules flexible in special circumstances for specific people?

Are decision-making processes clear? Do they follow a transparent procedure and is there an opportunity to step in and change this procedure?

Achievement

Does the organisation have a task-first or people-first culture? Is competition a driving force or is higher value placed on collaboration to achieve results? Do organisational initiatives and reward, commission or bonus systems inspire competition or cooperation?

***

To access a worksheet with these questions and more please see details on the page opposite.

Awareness is the first step and key to discussing contrasting styles of 'the way we do things around here'. Can you assess the positive impact of different orientations on the cultural values scales in your organisation? Providing clarity and guidance on how things are done in your space will go a long way to building a strong foundation of understanding. As with all of my suggestions, know that it is a process, an ongoing journey. We never quite arrive at the end point of learning.

When you engage in cultural dialogue with your teams, be clear about your goals and communicate openly. Maintain a neutral position – one that truly seeks to nurture diversity and promote inclusivity, leaving all judgement at the door. Gaining trust is key to the success of your diversity and inclusion initiatives. Good intention alone will not suffice. If you do not have the skills or experience to facilitate such dialogue, seek the support of a professional facilitator with expertise in cultural intelligence.

WANT TO KNOW MORE?

My online toolkit includes exclusive resources available to readers of *Curious about Culture*. These offer the opportunity for further exploration to facilitate deeper personal thinking and dialogue with others. To access these resources please visit: **rabbanicollective.com/curiousaboutculturetoolkit**. Please use the password 'I am curious' when prompted.

If you would like to go a step further beyond reliance on self-assessment, you can choose to take a formal assessment.

Cultural values profile

In part III of this book when we explored the six cultural value dimensions, we relied upon your self-awareness to arrive at some understanding of your cultural preferences. If you would like to more comprehensively uncover your orientation against these values, you can choose to take a cultural values assessment. This measures individual preferences that influence approaches to life and work across four cultural value dimensions in addition to the six value dimensions that you have discovered in this book.

Cultural intelligence profile

Earlier in the book, I described CQ as a form of intelligence that can be developed and measured. If you work across cultural differences including time zones and borders, and are committed to developing your cross-cultural effectiveness, this assessment can be particularly useful to you.

Let's talk

Whether you want to know more about customised training and coaching solutions to meet your personal or business objectives, or you are seeking a personalised and in-depth profile, or perhaps you have feedback on this book in your hand, I would love to hear from you. Please join the conversation via Facebook or LinkedIn, or send me an email message.

gaiti@rabbanicollective.com

facebook.com/RabbaniCollective

linkedin.com/company/rabbani-collective

REFERENCES AND FURTHER READING

Preface

Australian Bureau of Statistics (2020), 'Population', abs.gov.au/population.

Part I: Culture

Chapter 1: The cultural quotient

Hofstede, G (2011), 'Dimensionalizing Cultures: The Hofstede Model in Context', *Online Readings in Psychology and Culture*, 2(1).

Hall, ET (1976), *Beyond Culture*, Anchor Books.

Chapter 2: The cultural mirror

Adesina, Z & Marocico, O (2017), 'Is it easier to get a job if you're Adam or Mohamed?', BBC Inside Out, bbc.com/news/uk-england-london-38751307.

Association of Executive Search and Leadership Consultants (AESC), 'Checking your blind spot: ways to find and fix unconscious bias', aesc.org/insights/magazine/article/checking-your-blind-spots.

Banaji, MR (2016), *Blindspot: Hidden Biases of Good People*, Bantam.

Kahneman, D (2012), *Thinking, Fast and Slow*, Penguin Press.

Chapter 3: The cultural perspective

Australian College of Nursing (2019), 'Men in Nursing: Why it's okay for men to care', acn.edu.au/nurseclick/men-in-nursing-why-its-okay-for-men-to-care.

Cruickshank, V et al. (2018), 'Towards a measure of gender-related challenges faced by male primary teachers', *Australian Journal of Education*, vol. 62, no. 1, pp. 49–60.

Australian Government Workplace Gender Equality Agency (2019), 'Gender equitable recruitment and promotion', wgea.gov.au/data/wgea-research/gender-equitable-recruitment-and-promotion.

Gaudiano, P (2020), 'Here Is Why Diversity And Inclusion Are Disconnected, And How To Fix That', Forbes, forbes.com/sites/paologaudiano/2020/05/04/here-is-why-diversity-and-inclusion-are-disconnected-and-how-to-fix-that/?sh=4a8cd762fdd8.

Molenberghs, P & Louis, WR (2018), 'Insights From fMRI Studies Into Ingroup Bias', Frontiers in Psychology, frontiersin.org/articles/10.3389/fpsyg.2018.01868/full.

Part II: Cultural filters

Livermore, D (2015), *Leading with Cultural Intelligence: The Real Secret to Success*, AMACOM Books.

Chapter 4: The gender view

Hofstede Insights, 'National culture', hi.hofstede-insights.com/ national-culture.

Guterres, A (2020), 'Remarks to 64th Commission on the Status of Women', un.org/sg/en/content/sg/speeches/2020-03-09/ remarks-64th-commission-status-of-women.

National Geographic (2017), 'Where Women Reign: An Intimate Look Inside a Rare Kingdom', nationalgeographic.com/ photography/proof/2017/08/portraits-of-chinese-Mosuo-matriarchs.

Chapter 5: The generational outlook

Centre for Generational Kinetics, genhq.com.

Chapter 6: The filter of faith

The Church of Jesus Christ of Latter-Day Saints (2012), 'The Mormon Ethic of Community', newsroom.churchofjesuschrist. org/article/the-mormon-ethic-of-community.

Chapter 8: The language code

Boroditsky, L (2001), 'Does Language Shape Thought?: Mandarin and English Speakers' Conceptions of Time', *Cognitive Psychology*, vol. 43, pp. 1–22.

Battistella, EL (2014), *Sorry about that: The language of public apology*, Oxford University Press.

Chapter 9: The national dimension

Woodard, C (2012), *American Nations: A History of the Eleven Rival Regional Cultures of North America*, Penguin Books.

Mayberry, K (2016), 'Third Culture Kids: Citizens of everywhere and nowhere', BBC, bbc.com/worklife/article/20161117-third-culture-kids-citizens-of-everywhere-and-nowhere.

Part III: Cultural value dimensions

The Cultural Intelligence Center, culturalq.com.

Ronen, SS & Shenkar, O (1985), 'Clustering Countries on Attitudinal Dimensions: A Review and Synthesis', *The Academy of Management Review*, vol. 10, no. 3, pp. 435–454.

Chapter 10: Identity

Cherry, K (2020), 'Individualistic Cultures and Behavior', Verywellmind, verywellmind.com/what-are-individualistic-cultures-2795273.

Chapter 11: Authority

Zhou, C (2020), 'Why are Western countries being hit harder than East Asian countries by coronavirus?', *ABC News*, abc.net.au/news/2020-04-24/coronavirus-response-in-china-south-korea-italy-uk-us-singapore/12158504.

Chapter 12: Expression

Goleman, D (1995), *Emotional Intelligence*, Bantam Books.

Chapter 13: Communication

Goldberg, B (2019), 'Before your next presentation or speech, here's the first thing you must think about', TED, ideas.ted.com/before-your-next-presentation-or-speech-heres-the-first-thing-you-must-think-about.

ABOUT THE AUTHOR

Gaiti epitomises cultural diversity. She has lived and worked on three continents and travelled extensively over her 30 year career, working across diverse cultures. She has a rich appreciation of cultures, philosophies and people.

Of British-Asian heritage, Gaiti raised her third-culture daughter as a single parent in Dubai while climbing to the senior-most ranks in the Dubai Government.

She is the founder and managing director of Rabbani Collective, a company that delivers quantum improvement in business outcomes by leveraging the potential of people. As a Certified Cultural Intelligence Professional with the Cultural Intelligence Center and a Certified Results Based Coach, she is well-positioned to deliver relatable and actionable insights through bespoke learning and development programs.

When she is not immersed with her clients, she can be found in close embrace with new and exciting cultures across the globe, expressing her passion for Argentine tango and journalling her personal cross-cultural experiences.

She lives in Sydney with her Hong Kong-raised, Sri Lankan-born partner.

ACKNOWLEDGEMENTS

I cannot go to print without acknowledging the following people who have supported me on this writing journey:

- the researchers, journalists and fellow consultants whose bodies of work I refer to, for augmenting my perspectives
- my life partner, Wimal, for his ever-curious nature and gracious wisdom that inspire me to be the best version of myself
- my beautiful daughter and best friend Zehra who relentlessly cheers me on
- my writing buddies who pushed me through moments of doubt and encouraged me to find my voice as an author. You know who you are.

Many thanks also to the Cultural Intelligence Center (CQ Center) for allowing me to utilise their cultural value preference framework. The six cultural values explored in part III of this book are based on a list of 10 compiled by the CQ Center. Based on a comprehensive review of the literature, the CQ Center created this composite list of individual cultural value orientations and 10 cultural groupings or geographical clusters drawn from frameworks advanced by different research teams around the world – including, for example, Ang et al., 2003; Bluedorn et al, 1999; Bond et al., 1982; Dorfman & Howell, 1988; Gelfand et al., 2011; Hall, 1959, 1989; Hofstede, 1984, 2011; House et al., 2004 (GLOBE); Kirkman et al., 2006, 2017; Kluckhohn & Strodtbeck, 2002; Leung et al, 1995, 2005; Matsumoto et al., 2008; Nardon & Steers, 2009; Schwartz, 2006; Triandis, 1989, 2018; Trompenaars & Hampden-Turner, 1998; Wagner & Moch, 1986; Simcha Simi Ronen and Oded Shenkar, 1985; and others.

INDEX

China 13, 20, 30, 57, 71, 90, 91, 113, 118-119, 120
Christianity 47
Civil Rights Act 1964 38
Cold War 39
collectivism 83-87
Columbine massacre 37
communication 103-108, 139
community 45, 46-47
competitive 117-122
Confucianism 90, 119
context 103-108
cooperative 117-122
COVID-19 pandemic 36, 37, 90, 111-112
Cruickshank, Dr Vaughan 18
cultural intelligence (CQ) 3, 142
Cultural Intelligence Center (CQ Center) xv, 79, 81, 141
culture
– definition 3-5
curiosity 127-129

Denmark 118
diversity 19-21
Dubai x, 36, 73-74, 84, 105, 118

education 53-59, 134
El Norte 70

emotional intelligence (EQ) 3, 99
England xi, 13, 36, 48, 64, 70, 71, 72, 99, 113
English 61-62
– Australian 65
– British 64-65
– South African 65
expression 97-101, 139
eye contact 7, 8

faith 45-52, 133-134
Farsi 63
femininity 27
Fidel Castro 39
Finland 99
Fletcher School 90
football 72
formality 62
French 62, 63

Gaudiano, Paolo 20
gender 27-34, 132-133
– equality 29-32
– grammatical 63-64
– spectrum 32
Generation X 38
Generation Y 37-38
Generation Z 37
generations 35-43, 133
German 54

Martin Luther King Jr 38, 39
masculinity 18, 27
Middle East 113
Millennials 37-38
Mormonism 48-50
Mosuo 30
Munich Olympics 38

National Geographic 30
nationality 69-76, 135-136
Netherlands, the 99, 113
New Mexico 70
New York 71
New Zealand 91, 106
Nikkei cuisine 72
Northeast 71
Norway 28
nursing 18

Orwell, George 35
Oxford English Dictionary 66

Pakistan 12, 13-15, 48, 84
particularism 111-115
Peru 72
Philadelphia 71
Philippines, the 91
Port Arthur massacre 36, 37
Portuguese 63
Post-Millennials 37
power 139
power distance 89-94

prejudice 12-13
Princess Diana 36

Queensland xi

Ramadan 48
Romance languages 63
Ronen, Simcha Simi 81
rules 111-115, 139-140
Russia 91, 113
Ryerson University 12

Saudi Arabia 30
Scandinavia 28, 91, 113
Shenkar, Oded 81
Silent Generation 38-39
silo mentality 22
Singapore 55, 57, 90, 91
South Africa 71, 85
Spain 98
Spanish 61, 63-64
Sri Lanka 14, 15
Stanford University 61
stereotypes 13
Sufism 47
Sweden 90, 98, 99, 118
Switzerland 113
Sydney xi, 70

tango 32-33
teachers, primary school 18
Texas 70

thinking types 15-16

Thinking, Fast and Slow 15

third culture kids 74

Thoreau, Henry David xiv

Tiffany & Co. 31

Traditionalists 38-39

Tufts University 90

Turkey 113

UAE 48

United Arab Emirates (UAE)
xi, 11, 73-74, 92

United Kingdom xi, 13, 36,
48, 64, 70, 71, 72, 99, 113

United States 64, 70-71, 85,
113, 117

universalism 111-115

University of Tasmania 18

University of Toronto 12

Urdu 63

values 78-80, 141-142

Van Reken, Ruth 74

Wagstaffe, James 107

Washington D.C. 71

wasta 112

WeChat 41

West Coast 71

WhatsApp 41

Woodward, Colin 70

work/life balance 39-40

World Economic Forum 12

World Trade Center 35

World War II 38, 39

Zhuji 118

major st
PUBLISHING

We hope you enjoy reading this book. We'd love you to post a review on social media or your favourite bookseller site. Please include the hashtag #majorstreetpublishing.

Major Street Publishing specialises in business, leadership, personal finance and motivational non-fiction books. If you'd like to receive regular updates about new Major Street books, email info@majorstreet.com.au and ask to be added to our mailing list.

Visit majorstreet.com.au to find out more about our books and authors.

We'd love you to follow us on social media.

in linkedin.com/company/major-street-publishing

f facebook.com/MajorStreetPublishing

📷 instagram.com/majorstreetpublishing

🐦 @MajorStreetPub